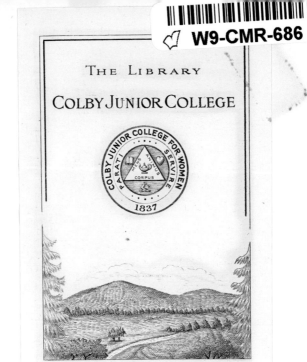

STUDIES IN MODERN EUROPEAN LITERATURE
AND THOUGHT

General Editor:
ERICH HELLER
Professor of German
in the University College of Swansea

ORTEGA Y GASSET

Also published in this Series

Arturo Barea: UNAMUNO
E. K. Bennett: STEFAN GEORGE
Roy Campbell: LORCA
J. M. Cocking: PROUST
Hugh Garten: GERHART HAUPTMANN
Rayner Heppenstall: LÉON BLOY
Hans Egon Holthusen: RILKE
P. Mansell Jones: BAUDELAIRE
Martin Jarrett-Kerr: FRANÇOIS MAURIAC
Janko Lavrin: GONCHAROV
Rob Lyle: MISTRAL
Richard March: KLEIST
Iris Murdoch: SARTRE
L. S. Salzberger: HÖLDERLIN
Elizabeth Sewell: PAUL VALÉRY
Cecil Sprigge: BENEDETTO CROCE
Enid Starkie: ANDRÉ GIDE
J. P. Stern: ERNST JÜNGER
Anthony Thorlby: FLAUBERT
E. W. F. Tomlin: SIMONE WEIL
Martin Turnell: JACQUES RIVIÈRE
Bernard Wall: ALESSANDRO MANZONI

Other titles in preparation

ORTEGA Y GASSET

AN OUTLINE OF HIS PHILOSOPHY

BY

JOSÉ FERRATER MORA

NEW HAVEN
YALE UNIVERSITY PRESS
1957

B
4568
O78
F4

11/26/59 C 472 8.65

ACKNOWLEDGMENT

Professor Milton C. Nahm, of Bryn Mawr College, has read this work in manuscript and has made extremely helpful suggestions concerning both content and presentation. I wish to assure him of my sincere gratitude.

JOSÉ FERRATER MORA

Bryn Mawr College.
April, 1955.

CONTENTS

I. Introduction . . . . page 9

II. Objectivism 15

III. Perspectivism 25

IV. Ratio-vitalism 38

    (a) The concept of vital reason 38

    (b) The doctrine of man 46

    (c) The doctrine of society 55

    (d) The idea of philosophy 60

I

Introduction

A short book on Ortega y Gasset's work and thought is a difficult undertaking if only for one reason: the astonishing range of Ortega's[1] intellectual interests. Ortega is, in the best sense of the word, a versatile writer. True, the Spanish philosopher has written neither novels nor plays and has almost invariably been loyal to one literary genre: the essay. Within this frame, however, there has been practically no subject upon which he has not touched. Skimming through the 3500-odd pages of his complete works, we find a staggering variety of writings: philosophical studies, articles on literary criticism, political essays and speeches, landscape descriptions, and historical interpretations. If we glance casually through the index of names appended to the collection of his works, we are no less impressed by the author's versatility; Renan and Einstein, Caesar and Husserl, Kant and Goya, Proust and Abenkhaldun are only some of the many men not only occasionally mentioned or quoted but discussed at some length. Some of the essays are unclassifiable. One, for example, is about the frame of a painting; another is a preface to a still unwritten book. Among the more conventional essays, it is not unusual for the author merely to broach the subject announced; considerable time is spent in preliminary or tangential considerations. As for the topics discussed, they seem to be unbounded. Ortega has written on the fountains in Nürnberg, on the French language, on the Gioconda, on the Russian ballet, on African ethnology and, of course, on history, love and metaphysics. In view of these facts, we may be inclined to believe that Ortega's variety of topics is either a mark of frivolity or an omen of superficiality. But the more carefully we look at the strokes of the brush, the more consistent and organized appears to be the picture.

This does not mean that Ortega is a systematic philosopher. Nor does he, we hope, pretend to be one. The emphasis that has been placed by both his followers and opponents on his 'system' or on his 'lack of system' is false. Ortega's is certainly no philosophical system of the Hegelian type. It is true that Ortega himself has made occasional remarks about his 'philosophical system',

[1] Throughout this book we shall use the name 'Ortega' instead of 'Ortega y Gasset', 'Ortega' being, according to Spanish usage, the philosopher's surname and playing thus the rôle of the English last name.

but the word 'system', like the word 'being' according to Aristotle, has an analogical rather than a univocal meaning. Its meaning in Ortega is not, certainly, the 'strong' one—the meaning a system takes on when it is almost completely formalized. But it is not the 'weak' one either—the meaning it takes on when reduced to a style of writing or to a relatively uniform method of approach. It has a somewhat subtler meaning, depending both on cogency of thoughts and recurrence of themes. If Ortega is said therefore, to have a 'system', it must be added that it is an *open* rather than a *closed* one.

In the present book we shall be primarily concerned with some of the most obvious features of Ortega's 'open system'. We shall, in other words, give a brief and somewhat sketchy account of his philosophy. We assume accordingly that Ortega's work, in spite of its diversity of subjects, its complexity, its 'allusions and elisions', [1] is chiefly of a philosophical nature, with all its elements organized around a core of philosophical assumptions. Now the word 'philosophy' is as ambiguous as the word 'system'. After all, the term 'system' has a commonly accepted, if vague, connotation—you cannot have a system unless you have a certain 'order'—while the term 'philosophy' seems to possess no universally accepted meaning except the one based upon the fact that the most extraordinary variety of human thoughts are usually recorded in books pretending to be philosophical. The student of philosophy has always been a little distressed to learn that Marcus Aurelius and John Stuart Mill are equally to be considered as philosophers. As his familiarity with the history of philosophy increases, so will his distress, for there was a time when

[1] José Ortega y Gasset, *Obras completas*, Madrid: Revista de Occidente, VI, 344 (1932). The arabic numerals inside parentheses designate the date of first publication, either in periodical or in book form. Quotations will follow the 1946–1947 edition of *Obras completas*, except for a few books not included therein or published at a later date. If an English translation in book form is available, it will be mentioned in brackets. It should be noted that English titles do not always correspond to Spanish ones and that sometimes, as in the case of the English translation of *España invertebrada (Invertebrate Spain)*, some other texts have been added to the one providing the title of the book. Information on the contents of English translations, as well as on the contents of *Obras completas*, is appended at the end of this volume. Most of our quotations will be mere references to *some* of the places where Ortega has developed the subjects dealt with in our book. Literal quotations will be restricted to a minimum, since the present writer believes that the thought of a philosopher cannot be adequately presented by means of an anthology of his writings.

practically all human intellectual endeavours, provided they were formulated at a reasonably reflective level, were regarded as philosophical. When classifying the work of an author as philosophy, we must, therefore, be cautious and provide a minimum of clarification of the meaning carried by such an ambiguous word.

Ortega's philosophy is extremely difficult to classify, because our writer is one of the very few in modern history who has noted with perfect clarity the problematic character of philosophical activity. We shall clarify this point later, and, for the time being, just say that Ortega's philosophy cannot be presented in a pedantically academic manner.

The first problem it raises is the choice of a suitable method of presentation. A number of methods are available, but none of them seems to be altogether satisfactory. If too much attention is focused upon the unity of Ortega's thought, we incur the risk of losing the flavour of its variety. If we insist too much on the diversity of subjects, sight may be lost of the one continuous stream of thought running through all of them. Ortega himself, however, has provided an answer to our problem. He has said that the only way to approach the question of human reality is the narrative way. Accordingly, the right method of explaining Ortega's philosophy would be the biographical one. Now, 'biographical method' is an expression that must be given a precise meaning. It would be a mistake to interpret it in the usual fashion, as if it consisted of a mere enumeration of facts arranged in chronological order. In Ortega's sense of the word, 'biography' is almost a technical term, indicating the peculiar 'systematic' structure of human life and human achievements. From this point of view, the use of a biographical method involves a certain understanding of the whole of that reality to which it is applied. We are here confronted, incidentally, with one of the perplexing vicious circles so frequent in non-formalistic philosophies. In order to understand a system of thought we must describe its various stages, but in order to understand each one of the stages we must have a certain idea, however vague, of the whole system. This method is, in fact, the one we commonly use when attempting to understand the significance of a particular human life: the early stages in a person's life help us to understand the later ones, but it is only its later stages that provide us with a basis for the interpretation of the earlier ones; and although these two modes of explanation are not exactly alike, the first concentrating more on the cause-effect relation and the second more on the whole-part relation, we use them simultaneously. They are indeed not really separate methods but part of the same one. It is the method we shall employ throughout the present book.

This biographical method will allow us to discuss now and then certain typically Ortegean topics that a more formal method would rule out of the picture. Furthermore, the biographical method makes it easier to give an adequate, if brief, account of some of the external circumstances that have prompted Ortega's most significant philosophical and literary creations. We shall, however, limit the application of the method to an outline of some fundamental stages or phases in Ortega's intellectual development.

The first may be taken to extend from 1902 to 1914, the second from 1914 to 1923, the third from 1924 to 1955. It may prove convenient to attach a name to each phase, even if we recognize that such a label is more a mnemonic device than a defining category.

The first phase we shall label *objectivism*. Ortega himself has given occasion for adopting such a label if we remember that in a preface (1916) to his volume *Persons, Works, Things* (*Personas, Obras, Cosas*) he recognized how one-sided his earlier objectivism was and how befitting it would be to emphasize again subjectivism stripped of its nineteenth-century connotations[1]. Although the preface in question was written in 1916, we can easily perceive a change in his book *Meditations on Quixote* (*Meditaciones del Quijote*) (1914)[2] and perhaps even earlier. As a matter of fact, some of the intellectual seeds that will bear fruit much later can be traced as early as 1910, and much that will be recognized as typically Ortegean makes its first appearance in two articles published in 1904 and reprinted only in 1946[3].

The second phase we shall label *perspectivism*. Some doctrines other than this can, of course, be detected during the period 1914-1923, but the above label provides a convenient designation for the entire phase. A noteworthy difference between the objectivist and the perspectivist stages is that, while the former contains much that will never again recur, the latter is an essential ingredient of the third period. The label arises out of the first essay in *The Spectator* (*El Espectador*),[4] but the doctrine of the *modi res considerandi* set forth in the *Meditations* may be held as an earlier formulation of it. Perspectivism can be considered from two angles: as a doctrine and as a method. The

---

[1] I, 419–20 (1916).
[2] I, 309–400 (1914).
[3] I, 13–18 (1904); I, 19–27 (1904).
[4] II, 15–21 (1916).

two combine frequently and the reader is sometimes left in doubt about the rôle that perspectivism plays in the whole system.

The third phase we shall label *ratio-vitalism*, a shorthand description used by Ortega himself[1]. It will prove to be Ortega's main achievement in philosophy. We fix 1924 as a beginning date because in that year Ortega's article 'Neither Vitalism nor Rationalism' ('Ni vitalismo ni racionalismo') was published. But we might also go back to 1923, the date of the publication of a major work containing ratio-vitalistic assumptions: *The Modern Theme* (*El tema de nuestro tiempo*). However, in this book, as if reacting against a widespread contemporary 'culturalism', Ortega emphasized the theme of life far more than his own doctrine of vital reason would permit. We shall consequently rule this work out of the third period and study it instead as the crowning point of the second. Needless to say, the third period will provide us with most of the themes that have come to be viewed as characteristically Ortegean. It is not only the longest phase in Ortega's life and work but also the most philosophical of all, or at least the one when the Spanish philosopher has been more insistent upon the 'technical' aspects of philosophy. We shall devote to it, therefore, relatively more space than to any of the others, and we shall interpret the first two in the light of the third. Now the presentation of the third period will gain in clarity if we divide it into a number of themes. These will be: (a) The concept of vital reason; (b) the doctrine of man; (c) the doctrine of society, and (d) the idea of philosophy. Thus unity will be achieved without necessarily eschewing diversity. In this way we expect to give a fairly complete, although by no means exhaustive account of Ortega's philosophy.

The present book is intended for a non-Spanish-speaking public. It will accordingly be impossible to avoid mentioning a few facts that Spanish readers are likely to take for granted. As a result, interpretation will often be accompanied by mere information. On the the other hand, certain questions intriguing to the Spanish-speaking public cannot be discussed here. We shall pay little attention, for example, to the problem of whether Ortega's claims of having long since foreshadowed many later philosophical developments in contemporary thought can be substantiated. Ortega is probably more original than his detractors proclaim and less original than his adherents preach, but the achievements of a philosopher must be measured in terms of truth rather than originality. We shall also ignore the question of

[1] VI, 196, note (1934) [*Concord and Liberty*, henceforth called *Concord*, p. 164].

whether ideas *not* playing a central rôle in Ortega's philosophy are faulty. We can see little purpose in noticing that Ortega's considerations on Debussy's music[1] are contradicted by facts, or in remarking that his interpretation of Quine's statement, 'There must always be undemonstrable mathematical truths',[2] is a misinterpretation. We are not concerned with errors irrelevant to the central themes; some distorted facts or some questionable reasonings may very well be lodged in an interesting and even sound philosophy. We shall indulge in neither bickering nor applause, but try to keep close to the spirit of a famous apophthegm: Neither bewail nor rejoice, but understand.

[1] II, 236–46 (1921).
[2] V, 528 (1941) [*Concord*, p. 62].

II

Objectivism

From 1902 to 1913 Ortega published no book, but his name began
to be known among Spaniards as the author of a number of
noteworthy articles. These articles were occasionally published in
literary magazines—*Vida Nueva*, *La Lectura*, *Europa*, etc.—and
very often in a daily newspaper, *El Imparcial*. The last fact deserves consideration. It has been, of course, quite common for
Spanish writers to publish articles in newspapers. Not a few of
the best examples of Spanish literature in the nineteenth and
twentieth centuries first appeared in daily journals. But Ortega
has always shown an extreme predilection for newspapers—at
least of a certain type—and has been associated in various ways,
and not merely as an occasional contributor, with some of the
outstanding Spanish daily journals: *El Imparcial* first, then *El
Sol*, and finally *Crisol* and *Luz*. It was said of him that he was
born 'on a rotary printing press'. Since 1936 he has often com-
plained of 'not having a paper', meaning a paper where he could
without restraint set up rules of intellectual policy. Ortega has
been a newspaperman *par excellence*, in a sense almost forgotten
to-day even in countries where newspapers still play an important cultural and educational rôle. On the other hand, he has
provided newspapers with a type of literature that has been
truly exceptional, even taking into consideration the high intellectual standards of some of the Spanish and Spanish-Ameri-
can newspapers[1]. We do not for a moment forget that other
Spanish thinkers, such as Unamuno, Maeztu, d'Ors, have given
to daily journals half, if not more, of their intellectual production.
But Ortega has tried to introduce through the medium of
newspapers not only ideological issues or cultural information
but also a certain amount of academic, if highly polished,
philosophical clarification. His tendency to inundate the Sunday
issues with philosophical literature has been growing steadily
during the second and third of the aforementioned periods. To
give *some* examples: a series of articles on the question 'What is
knowledge?' in all likelihood derived from his university lectures,
came out in *El Sol's* Sunday feuilleton sometime in the thirties[2];
an article on 'Leibniz and Metaphysics' was published in *La*

---

[1] Ortega has also contributed to some fine newspapers in Spanish
America, principally *La Nación* of Buenos Aires.
[2] Not included in *Obras completas*. See *El Sol*, February-March, 1931.

Nación in the twenties[1]; his most publicized book, *The Revolt of the Masses* (*La rebelión de las masas*), was delivered for the first time to the public in the form of newspaper articles from 1926 on[2]. We certainly do not wish to give the reader the impression that everything written by Ortega has come out in the same fashion. Essays in literary magazines, articles in learned journals, and also formal books account for a substantial part of his production. But on the whole publication in newspapers has been, as it were, a 'constant' in Ortega's way of communicating his thoughts to the public. Such a fact is not lightly to be dismissed. Two reasons may be adduced to account for it. One is Ortega's personal fondness for this form of literary activity, a fondness helped, if not brought forth, by the attraction he felt for a new subject as soon as another had been broached. The other reason was emphasized by Ortega's best disciple, Julián Marías, when he remarked that Ortega *had* to use ostentatious public media of communication[3]. We shall briefly follow Marías' account of Ortega's reason for choosing such media, inasmuch as it will help us to understand some of the Spanish philosopher's aims, at least during the first period of his intellectual activity.

The substance of Marías' argument, to which we shall add some of our own reflexions, runs as follows. When Ortega began writing, Spanish culture was still suffering from nineteenth-century intellectual indigence. The so-called generation of 1898 had already revived Spain's spiritual nerve, but ideas, and in particular philosophical ideas, seemed still to lack either actuality or rigour. Most of the current literary output was either pure literature—and often very fine literature, indeed—or mere erudition. Exceptions to this rule might, of course, be found, but even these had to breathe in a rather murky ideological atmosphere. The first one to try to clear it was Miguel de Unamuno. But Unamuno, who left nothing to be desired as to seriousness of purpose and breadth of information, cared little for rigour. As we have shown elsewhere,[4] his aim as a writer with regard to his public may be summed up in one word: stimulation. Inspiration

---

[1] III, 431–34 (1926).
[2] IV, 141–278 (1930) [*The Revolt of the Masses*, henceforth called *Revolt, passim*].
[3] J. Marías, *Ortega y la idea de la razón vital*, Santander-Madrid. Colección 'El Viento Sur', 1948, pp. 13–24. Also VI, 353 (1932). For an opinion on books 'as falsifications', III, 447 (1927).
[4] José Ferrater Mora, *Unamuno: bosquejo de una filosofía*, Buenos Aires: Losada, 1945; 2nd. revised and enlarged edition, Buenos Aires: Sudamericana, 1956.

rather than argument had been his driving power. The fact that we acknowledge to-day in Unamuno's works and deeds a great deal of what has become an essential part of European contemporary philosophy does not prevent us from admitting that his aims were quite different from Ortega's. The latter aspired to inject into Spanish culture an ingredient it badly needed: thoughtfulness. In an intellectually enlightened atmosphere Ortega might have done what was being done at the same time by other European philosophers: Bergson, Husserl or Bertrand Russell. In other words, he might have limited himself to working out a core of philosophical intuitions and delivering them to a restricted public by the usual means: papers read before learned societies, contributions to scholarly journals, lectures in universities. But what if learned societies are few, scholarly journals practically non-existent, universities dominated by routine? Was it not therefore much better to take a roundabout course? Would not a long detour avoid the pitfalls of a shortcut? What has in fact happened is that Ortega's encircling method has been highly responsible for giving form and substance to the Spanish intellectual atmosphere. Thus we can understand his renunciation of specialization and his choice of newspapers as the chief medium of public communication.

There is, however, another reason for Ortega's choice. Ortega is not only a philosopher; he is also, and in large measure, a writer. He belongs to the group of twentieth-century Spanish authors who have offered Spain a new Golden Age in literature. This new Golden Age is dominated by a poetic sensitivity that permeates a good many pages written in the last fifty years. As it has been said, twentieth-century Spanish prose is more 'poetic' than nineteenth-century Spanish poetry[1]. Now the word 'poetic' must be understood here as meaning something other than the vague language of feeling. It designates above all a recognition of a writers's commitment in his use of language. The problem of language, rather than the problem of rhetorical expression—or, in the case of the poets, of technical versification—has been, indeed, predominant with all these writers. Ortega has certainly been no outsider to this revival. No doubt, his preoccupation was philosophical thought; but he has also created a new style. This style is not free from mannerism. It is hard to understand why, in the middle of a very able exposition of Max Weber's

[1] See Pedro Salinas, *Literatura española siglo XX*, México: Séneca, 1941, pp. 59–82; 2nd. enlarged edition, México: Robredo, 1949, pp. 34–44.

ideas on the decadence of the Roman Empire, a passage is inserted in which the author, supposedly writing by the sea-shore, compares the ocean to a huge crossbow and his own heart to an arrow[1]. Some of these mannerisms were unfortunately imitated by Spanish youngsters, and frequently Ortegean catchwords were substituted for real concepts. Yet there is no point in blaming Ortega for his brilliant style. At a time when intellectual production is marred by dullness, a brilliant style is far more refreshing than harmful. Literary craftmanship is indeed one of Ortega's outstanding accomplishments. Some of his best pages are his travel descriptions, which he himself regrets are too few[2]. Ortega's literary style is, however, always adapted to the thoughts he tries to convey to the reader. And thoughts are always the background, if not the foreground, of his written work. Even when description predominates over analysis, he seems anxious to take it only as a starting point for reflection[3]. No wonder Ortega has come to the defence of metaphorical expression as a valid tool of philosophical analysis[4]. Even if we think his ideas on this point somewhat far-fetched, we cannot help detecting therein the keen perception that a pure-bred writer has of the scope and limitations of his own instrument.

Ortega therefore started his career as a thinker by choosing a literary style and certain media of communication that were particularly apt to bring him into the limelight of the Spanish intellectual scene. All the writings we shall discuss in this section bear the mark of his unusual combination of literary skill and philosophical sagacity.

In these formative years the foremost theme is objectivism. In more than one passage Ortega assured the reader, and in particular young Spanish readers, that too much attention has been paid so far to human beings and too little to things or to ideas. We might choose a number of quotations; we shall limit ourselves

---

[1] II, 544 (1926).
[2] IV, 386 (1932).
[3] Outstanding examples are: II, 249–68 (1915) [fragmentary translation in *Invertebrate Spain*, pp. 103–15], where the description of a journey from Madrid to Asturias serves as a point of departure for an interpretation of Castile; II, 413–50 (1925) [*Op. cit.*, pp. 116–42], where along the thread of a trip through Castile he develops his ideas on liberalism and democracy; II, 553–60 (1915) [*Invertebrate Spain*, pp. 202–12], where a description of the Monastery of El Escorial is used as a frame for an essay on the idea of 'pure effort', with a comparison between Cervantes' *Don Quixote* and Fichte's philosophy.
[4] II, 387–400 (1924).

to a most revealing sentence. It is the one in which Ortega says that he cannot understand how it is possible for men to arouse more interest than ideas, and persons more than things; and he adds that an algebraic theorem or a huge old stone in the Guadarrama Sierra is more meaningful than all the employees in a government office[1]. He accordingly asks his fellow-citizens to get rid of 'the secret leprosy of subjectivity'[2]. It should be noted that a few years later a footnote was added to the above sentence stating that such an opinion is 'sheer blasphemy'. Nevertheless, this stress upon objectivity recurs in different ways and in different tones throughout the articles written during the 1904-1913 period.

There are many reasons for the adoption of the above intellectual policy. An obvious one is Ortega's reaction from a high-pressure personalistic atmosphere pervading Spanish life. The word 'personalistic' can, nevertheless, be understood in two ways: a superficial one, as the deplorable habit of a people wasting time on barren personal discussion, and a deep one, as the living basis of a community that has chosen *person* as the highest value in the universe[3]. We suspect that Ortega placed too much emphasis on the former and too little on the latter. This fact has been recognized, at least implicitly, by Ortega himself, for otherwise he would not have renounced his earlier opinions on this issue. Yet as a reaction against a certain state of affairs, those opinions were by no means groundless. On the other hand, in the very core of his objectivistic claims lies much that later became the link between the first and the second period.

Ortega went abroad to study philosophy. He spent several years in Germany, specially in Leipzig, Berlin and Marburg. In Marburg he studied under the guidance of Herman Cohen, the head of one of the two great neo-Kantian schools flourishing in Germany at the beginning of this century. Going abroad, in particular going to Germany, in order to study philosophy was not unusual in Spain. More than half a century before Ortega a great Spaniard, Julián Sanz del Río, went to Germany in search

[1] I, 443 (1909).
[2] I, 447 (1909). Also I, 87 (1908).
[3] A brilliant interpretation of this deep meaning of personalism can be found in Américo Castro's *The Structure of Spanish History*, Princeton: Princeton University Press, 1953, a translation of the second much revised and practically rewritten edition of his work *España en su historia*, Buenos Aires: Losada, 1948. Unamuno had followed a very similar path.

of new ideas. But as the pilgrims and the times were quite dissimilar, the two intellectual pilgrimages yielded quite different results. Sanz del Río imported into Spain a philosophical system that, while having gained but little credit in Europe, had conquered the hearts of a handful of brave and enthusiastic adherents: Krausism, the somewhat involved system of Karl Christian Friedrich Krause, a sincere and pedantic idealist. Sanz del Río very soon gave Krausism a Spanish turn, emphasizing its ethical, personalistic and absolutistic aspects. Ortega, on the contrary, did not import any philosophy. The system he followed for a time was the one then prevalent in the most sophisticated German circles. He preached, certainly, an intensive study of Kant, and he declared later that he had lived in a Kantian atmosphere, in a philosophical edifice that was at the same time a prison[1]. But he spread Kantianism, or rather neo-Kantianism, in a rather perfunctory way, more as a method of rigorous philosophizing than as a body of propositions. The result of Ortega's training, helped if not fostered by his own disposition, was thus the moulding of a critical spirit, allergic to received opinions, to intellectual clumsiness, to obsolete ideas. Again, this was not new in Spain. But Ortega carried to extremes an attitude that he has often summed up by means of one of his favourite phrases: to be abreast of the times[2]. He tried to become the spear-head of a new intellectual movement capable of sweeping away all that was shaky, rotten or dead in Spanish life and culture, but not necessarily all that was traditional. In a significant article, published as early as 1906, Ortega sharply attacked traditionalists, not because of their fondness for tradition but because of their inability to preserve tradition[3]. Traditionalists, he writes, want to carry the present back to the past. They have accordingly no regard for the past as such. If they loved it, they would certainly not attempt to petrify it. The living past, on the other hand, is rooted in the present and will survive in the future. Therefore, it would be a grave error to interpret Ortega's concern for the present and future as naïve anti-traditionalistic rhetoric. His struggle against the dead past is quite compatible with his insistence upon history, in exactly the same sense that his insistence upon the living future is quite consistent with his fight against utopia. However, the vigour with which he attempted to change routine intellectual habits was conspicuous. The

[1] IV, 25 (1924).
[2] IV, 156 (1930) [*Revolt*, p. 31]. The English translator writes: 'at the height of times'.
[3] I, 425-9 (1906). Also II, 43 (1911) and I, 363-5 (1914).

justification of the past as past occupied only a small part of his thoughts. Practically all of his thinking in this period concerned the main question: how can Spain be abreast of the times.

From the beginning of his intellectual career Ortega was therefore involved in the time-honoured struggle between *hispanizantes* (those who wanted to hispanicize everything and were reluctant to admit foreign habits or ideas) and *europeizantes* (who wanted to inject into Spain what was called, rather vaguely, *European civilization*). This distinction is, of course, misleading, because the words *hispanizante* and *europeizante* have more than one meaning. Granted this ambiguity, however, we can say that Ortega was, and has always remained, an *europeizante*. To be such in Ortega's sense of this term has little to do with the straight importation of foreign habits or of foreign techniques. Unlike a good many Spaniards of his time, Ortega was not dazzled by the brilliant side of modern industrial revolution and did not for a moment believe that the mere introduction of Western European techniques would automatically heal all Spanish ills. He welcomed modern techniques but warned that they were a by-product of something far more fundamental than technique: science, culture, education. Pure science in particular—including, of course, philosophy—he considered the root of European civilization[1]. Therefore, in order to change Spain into a European country, it was necessary, in his opinion, to turn away from all superficial cures based upon imitation. Let us not, he wrote in an early article, call simply for railways, industry or trade, and still less for European costumes. Let us rather strive for a way of civilization that, while being positively Spanish, can become at the same time fundamentally European[2]. The so-called 'Spanish problem' is thus a problem of discipline. Spaniards must no longer live in a state of unconsciousness. They must above all give up 'adamism', the fatal mistake of starting everything afresh without intellectual seriousness, continuity of purpose or cooperation. In fact, only on the basis of intellectual discipline will Spain become a 'European possibility'[3]. But in doing so, Spain will cease to be a passive reservoir of foreign thoughts and habits and will become instead a powerful source of European renovation. As he said later, in another context, the first thing to do in a national community is 'not to imitate'[4].

This attitude clashed, of course, rather violently with the opi-

[1] I, 102 (1908).
[2] I, 107 (1908).
[3] I, 138 (1910).
[4] *Rectificación de la República*, Madrid: Revista de Occidente, 1931.

nions of the out and out *hispanizantes*. Among the latter we may provisionally include Unamuno, although the word *hispanizante* is quite inadequate to typify Unamuno's attitude. Unamuno was not a hispanicist in the usual sense of the term. He shared with Ortega a horror of the conventional shallow Spanish traditionalism. Unamuno's hispanicism and anti-Europeanism were therefore of a more subtle character than he himself indulged in believing when launching such slogans as 'Let them [the Europeans] invent' or 'Europe is a shibboleth'. His notion of the 'eternal tradition' was clearly indicative of his abhorrence of the dead past. In order to divulge his views on the subject, however, Unamuno used a method that was closer to paradox than to reasoning. He declared, among other things, that if it was impossible for the same nation to bring forth both Descartes and Saint John of the Cross, he would rather retain the latter. This must be understood, of course, in the light of Unamuno's deep sense of personalism, and is in tune with his later proclamation that Saint Theresa's deeds are at least as worthy as any European institution or any *Critique of Pure Reason*. Now Ortega could not accept, and in his objectivistic period not even endure, such irritating paradoxes. The point is worth mentioning because it gives a clear picture of what Ortega stood for before watering down his own enthusiastic Europeanism. His opinions on the issue in question appeared most clearly in an article on 'Unamuno and Europe'[1], in which he emphatically declared that Unamuno —whom he praised in other respects and to whom he paid moving homage thirty years later[2]—was an obscurantist who introduced nothing but confusion. He even called him an *energúmeno*, a 'violent person'. In Ortega's opinion, it was in fact sheer confusionism to prefer Descartes to Saint John of the Cross, not because the great Spanish saint and poet was an unimportant figure, but because without Descartes—who was, according to Ortega, the key-figure in all modern European philosophy—we would remain in the dark and become incapable of understanding anything, including the 'brown sackcloth' of Juan de Yepes, the worldly name of the great mystic. The confusion was all the more unfortunate in that Unamuno was often hailed by Ortega as a very powerful mind and, indeed, as a mentor of the Spanish intelligentsia. Unamuno was, according to Ortega, one of the last bastions of Spanish hopes[3]. All this conceded, however, Ortega deemed it proper to substitute his

[1] I, 128–32 (1909).
[2] V, 264–5 (1937).
[3] I, 118 (1908).

'brand-new' thoughtful europeanism for Unamuno's paradoxical and harsh 'africanism'.

Against overemphasis on ideals—of all sorts—Ortega was thus insistent upon ideas—but not of all sorts. This point deserves further elucidation, for it marks the transition from objectivism to perspectivism. The link between these two phases lies in Ortega's shifting the emphasis from ideas at large to certain kinds of ideas. At the beginning of his philosophical and literary career Ortega was in fact so haunted by the need of intellectual discipline that he seemed prone to accept all ideas provided they had a modern European tinge. He even seemed to be willing to shirk many issues for the sake of a much needed virtue: clarity[1]. His arguments in favour of precision[2], both in thought and in volition, his fondness for 'system'[3], at least as a programme for the future, his strong dislike for the blending of literature and science, no matter how literary-minded he was himself—all this aimed at a revival of Spanish spiritual life based upon a great wealth of ideas. No wonder he was called a rationalist and even accused of intellectualism. Now intellectualism would be a very inadequate label for a philosopher who amidst his struggle for clear ideas never forgot that ideas, however abstract, must not be divorced from life. We shall see later that the relation between life and ideas is a central issue in Ortega's philosophy, one of his favourite tenets being that while ideas cannot be separated from life, life itself cannot exist without ideas. It may be pointed out that, *in nuce*, this position can already be detected in those early pages in which Ortega dismisses certain ideas in favour of certain others. As early as 1911[4] the Spanish philosopher claimed that if discipline—intellectual, moral and aesthetic discipline—is still what Spain needs most of all, such a discipline has a very definite purpose: to bring us back to 'the vital'[5]. We need, to be sure, ideas, but only 'essential' ideas[6]. We must, in other words, abandon idealism[7], which is a by-product of abstractionism.

---

[1] A restatement of this opinion is in VI, 351 (1932). See also *La redención de las provincias y la decencia nacional*, Madrid: Revista de Occidente, 1931.
[2] I, 113 (1908).
[3] I, 114 (1908).
[4] I, 551 (1911).
[5] I, 551 (1911).
[6] I, 209 (1911).
[7] 'Idealism' is used here and henceforward as a technical term, denoting a certain modern philosophical tendency, typified, among others, by Kant and in part by Descartes and Leibniz.

These opinions are all the more surprising because they were held at a time when Ortega still appeared to many to be advocating a sort of philosophical rationalism. They are, however, a mere sample of an attitude that, while being respectful toward reason, never allowed rationalism to lead the way. This is, incidentally, one of the reasons why Ortega, who had little reverence for German political rigidity and harshness—he was in favour of the Allies during World War I—felt more at ease with German 'vital culture' than with the polished civilization of the French. Germany, he claimed, had more to teach in the way of ideas, even if France had better things to offer by way of manners [1] and England more to give by way of political ability [2]. Very soon Ortega began to display a profound mistrust of any encroachments of pure reason upon life. He even appeared sometimes to go so far in this new direction that many people again mistook his position and interpreted it as an anti-intellectualistic vitalism. He was compelled to declare that both reason and life are one-sided, and that a new stand has to be taken by those who want to prevent either one from being absorbed by the other. However, the link between objectivism and perspectivism is to be found in this shift from the rational to the vital, or rather in this effort to restore life and reality in their own right. The method Ortega advocated most frequently in order to achieve that purpose is the perspectivistic method. In the light of it we shall try to account for Ortega's main tenets during the next, very active, phase of his intellectual development.

[1] I, 209 (1911).
[2] On English political ability see especially III, 450 (1927); IV, 293 (1937); and V, 261–3 (1937).

III

Perspectivism

Between 1914 and 1923 Ortega published a number of important books. They may be roughly classified in two groups. The first includes books of selected articles, essays, notes, meditations, etc., most of them previously printed in journals or newspapers. The second includes books dealing with, or at least centering upon, one topic. To the first group belong the three first volumes of the eight-volume series entitled *The Spectator (El Espectador*, I, 1916; II, 1917; III, 1921)[1]. To the second group belong three major works: *Meditations on Quixote*, hereinafter called *Meditations (Meditaciones del Quijote*, 1914), *Invertebrate Spain (España invertebrada*, 1921) and the book translated into English as *The Modern Theme (El tema de nuestro tiempo*, 1923). To these volumes a number of articles, which came out in book form only much later, should be added. On the whole this makes an impressive number of pages, swarming with questions, analyses, insights, flashes of wit and literary findings. It appears by no means easy to detect in them traces of a systematic philosophy.

Fortunately, we possess some sort of a philosophical programme at the very threshold of the *Meditations*. This book opens with a declaration of war upon any attempt to make the world of the philosopher a cloistered universe. Following a tendency that had been fostered by the German philosopher Georg Simmel and had increased through the years in some sections of European philosophy, Ortega claimed that no reality, however humble, and no question, however unusual, can be put aside by a truly alert philosopher. Not all realities and questions lie, of course, on the same level. At issue with the positivists' flat universe, Ortega has often asserted that hierarchy permeates reality[2]. But this does not preclude the fact that each reality has a depth of its own and that the philosopher's task is to penetrate its surface in order to peer into its hidden nature. Thus the method to be adopted stands out in sharp contrast to the favourite approach of traditional academic philosophy. Instead of dismissing our near-by realities as unworthy of notice, we must try rather to discover their meaning. As Ortega himself writes, we must raise each reality to the plenitude of its significance. This

[1] Although *Persons, Works, Things* was published in 1916 and belongs apparently to the first group, all of the essays and articles it contains were written and published in periodicals before 1914.
[2] I, 319, 321-2 (1914).

point deserves some attention. Since the advent of phenomenology and existentialism, we have fallen into the habit of reading philosophical works encumbered with analyses of realities that only thirty years ago would have been barred in academic circles as irrelevant if not impertinent. We have been taught again and again that no reality, however unacademic, is liable to escape the cutting edge of philosophical clarification. This situation has given cause for concern, and in some quarters the complaint has been heard that at this rate philosophy will soon dissolve into a hunting for minutiae or into high-sounding literature. But such complaints become pointless as soon as we discover that in many instances the elaborate analysis of unacademic themes has led to the core of the deepest philosophical questions. This open-door policy in philosophy was preached by Ortega at the beginning of his career and has since been consistently carried on by him against wind and tide. The variety of his intellectual interests appears thus in a new light. It is not a result of intellectual instability, or at least, not solely, but also a consequence of a philosophical attitude.

Ortega has given this attitude expression in different ways. One seems to be particularly adequate for our purpose. We may call it the theory of circumstances. At the beginning of his *Meditations* the Spanish writer claimed that man communicates with the universe by means of his circumstances[1]. He may try, and he has often tried, to do away with them, but no fruitful result has ever ensued from this attempt. Some people may prefer to look at the world *sub specie aeternitatis*. It is far more rewarding to look at it *sub specie circumstantiarum*, or, circumstances being after all temporal, *sub specie instantis*. In fact, no other method is available if we aim at a real, living universe instead of contenting ourselves with a spectral and dead one. Circumstances are not only the momentous realities and problems of the world we live in but also the seemingly humble things and questions that surround us at every moment of our existence. Therefore, it would be wrong, and even unfair, to dismiss them lightly. Circumstances are, so to speak, the umbilical cord that ties us to the rest of the universe. We must accept them as starting points and perhaps as landmarks of our philosophical inquiry. Circumstances, however, are more than our surrounding universe. They are also an essential element of our lives. Thus Ortega was soon led to formulate a sentence that later proved to be a corner-stone of his philosophy: 'I am myself

[1] I, 319 (1914).

26

and my circumstances'[1]. The phrase may sound trivial. In fact, it is not more trivial than most philosophical sentences are when we persist in taking them only at their face value. In Ortega's formula a self is identified with himself *and* his circumstances, and therefore the thesis is maintained—against idealist philosophers—that a self can never be postulated as an ontologically independent being. Far from being a trivial tautology, this phrase appears rather as an involved double assumption according to which I cannot conceive of myself without conceiving at the same time of my own circumstances and, conversely, I cannot conceive of any circumstances without conceiving of myself as their dynamic centre. Man is, in Ortega's conception, a 'circumstantial being'; whatever he does, he must do in view of his circumstances[2]. We shall ponder later over this question, which will prove to be decisive in our more formal presentation of Ortega's philosophical anthropology. At the present stage it will suffice to keep in mind that Ortega conceives of human circumstances as the natural and sole medium of every human being, as the thing we must unhesitatingly accept unless we resign ourselves to turn our real being into a pure abstraction. This is certainly in tune with some other contemporary philosophers who stand for an 'open world' against the 'closed universe' postulated by idealist thinkers. It must be remembered, however, that Ortega does not simply advocate a 'philosophy of the open world' but insists upon the *fact* that whatever your philosophy may be you cannot avoid living in such a world. As Kant began his *Critique of Pure Reason* by considering the *factum* of physical science, Ortega begins his philosophy by considering the *factum* of human life existing among circumstances.

Circumstances are thus a crude fact. They are not, however, an opaque reality. Contrary to the pervading irrationalism of our time, Ortega stresses again and again the need for rational clarity. True, such a need has always been acknowledged by most philosophers. The very existence of philosophy evinces a taste for rationality that is at the same time a perpetual quest for clarity. But Ortega's notion of clarity differs in some respects from the traditional one. Clarity is not something superimposed on life as if it were external to it. Neither is it life itself, but rather 'the plenitude of life'[3] or, in our already familiar vocabulary, life in the plenitude of its meaning. Hence the conception of

[1] I, 322 (1914).
[2] There is clearer restatement of this opinion in VI, 348 (1932).
[3] I, 358 (1914).

reason as a 'vital function'[1] that Ortega worked out later in detail and that appears already in the *Meditations*, coupled with the assertion that the usual state of war between reason and life must be looked at with suspicion. Now in order to attain such a plenitude two elements are needed: one is the *concept;* the other is the *perspective*.

Let us start with Ortega's notion of concepts. He has defined them in various ways. Concepts are not intended, for example, to serve as substitutes for the living impressions of reality[2]. In so far as we aim at the concrete reality of things, we cannot help living under the spur of our impressions. They are, as it were, the basic layer of our existence, the main body of our spontaneous life. To dismiss impressions as sources of error, as is done too often by idealists and rationalists, is only a subterfuge. Against mistrust of impressions and, in general, of vital spontaneity, Ortega proclaims the necessity of developing and even of cultivating them. To act otherwise is a fatal error or, still worse, sheer hypocrisy. Hence his insistence upon the need for attending to a great many segments of life usually disregarded by philosophers. In this respect Ortega fully agrees with Nietzsche's demand—and with Simmel's recommendation—to unfold the wings of life to the utmost. Science and justice, art and religion are not the sole realities worthy of man's thought and sacrifice. It would be highly desirable some day in the pantheon of illustrious men to have not only a genius in physics like Newton and a genius in philosophy like Kant but a 'Newton of pleasures' and a 'Kant of ambitions'[3]. Pleasures and ambitions must therefore be given their full scope. Contrary to Nietzsche though, Ortega does not believe that the layer of spontaneity, out of which impressions arise, is self-sufficient. It seems to be unbounded; actually, it has many limitations: among others, the fact that pure spontaneity, deprived of cultivation, is a blind and senseless force, 'full of sound and fury, signifying nothing'. In order to give it meaning, it is necessary to introduce concepts. In a statement reminiscent of a celebrated sentence of Kant, Ortega seems to imply that impressions without concepts are blind and concepts without impressions are shallow. Unlike Kant, however, he couples impressions and concepts as if they were two sides of the same reality. Here lies, incidentally, a source of difficulties for Ortega's philosophy: the same difficulties that have perennially baffled philosophers as soon as they have attempted to correlate sense

[1] I, 353 (1914).
[2] I, 318 (1914).
[3] I, 320 (1914).

impressions and ideas. Ortega does not overlook these difficulties, but he thinks he has found a clue to the solution by watering down both impressions and concepts, the former being in his opinion more than sense impressions and the latter being less than formal schemata. We are not going to take him to task for this solution, inasmuch as our purpose is to understand rather than to criticize. We shall simply point out that Ortega wavers between a definition of concepts as 'ideal schemata' and their characterization as pragmatic tools for grasping reality. At all events, he seems to be quite convinced that without concepts we should be at a loss amidst the whirlwind of impressions. Hence the importance attached to the process of conceptualization—an importance that is enhanced rather than lessened by the fact that, contrary to Hegel's opinion, concepts for him are not the metaphysical substance of reality. They are organs of perception in exactly the same sense that the eyes are organs of sight. But 'perception' must be understood here as 'perception of depth'[1] or perception of the order and connection of realities. Perceptions take us from the level of spontaneous life to the level of reflective life. Spontaneous life, however, is never laid aside; it is always the beginning and the end of our inquiry. We do not know whether Ortega would agree with the definition 'Concepts are good conductors of impressions', but we think it not too inaccurate a statement of his views on the subject.

Concepts are thus closer to life than most people would admit. They are also very close to that other notion often referred to as 'perspective'.

We can trace its origins as far back as 1910, when Ortega emphatically declared that there are as many entities as there are points of view[2]. This doctrine was at the time allied to two other theories, that according to which beings are reduced to values and that affirming that no entity can be said to exist unless related to other entities, so that what we call a thing is nothing but a bundle of relations. The former theory is substantially Platonic; the latter fundamentally Leibnizian. Ortega dropped both theories a few years later. In return, the 'doctrine of the point of view' was reasserted and developed on several occasions. Three of them will be mentioned here.

The first one was in the *Meditations*[3]. Contrary to traditional opinions that reality consists in matter or spirit or any other of the usual metaphysical constructions set up by philosophers,

[1] I, 350 (1914).
[2] I, 475 (1910).
[3] I, 321 (1914).

Ortega boldly puts forward the proposal that the ultimate substance of the world is a perspective. Now while in the former stage perspectivism was, as we noticed, dependent upon an abstract ontology of a relationistic type, in the present phase it is based in a large measure upon a will to concreteness which permeates the philosopher's *Meditations* from start to finish. No wonder therefore that we find on the same pages an attack on the conception of wholes as abstractions of parts and even a definition of the hammer as the abstraction of the sum of its strokes[1]. Nevertheless, the theory of perspective is still wrapped in the doctrine of circumstances and lacks the chiselling its author gave it later. Only in 1916, in an article entitled 'Truth and Perspective', included in the first volume of *The Spectator*, the doctrine of perspective is presented stripped of distracting incidental remarks. Ortega begins by raising the question of the old-established opposition between scepticism and dogmatism. Scepticism asserts that inasmuch as reality is split up into individual perspectives universal truths are unattainable. Dogmatism, and in particular rationalistic dogmatism, asserts that inasmuch as there are universal truths no individual perspective is ever possible. Now Ortega takes it as a *fact* that individual perspective is the only way of seizing reality and, therefore, of formulating universal truths. He is not unaware, of course, that such a perspectivism is an old-time honoured view in the history of philosophy. He quotes in this connection Leibniz, Nietzsche and Vaihinger; he might have quoted, too—to mention only a few—Teichmüller, Simmel or Russell. But he declares that his predecessors, while having similar aims, started from different assumptions. This seems quite clear as far as Nietzsche or Vaihinger is concerned. It appears less clear with regard to Leibniz. There is, however, in our opinion, a fundamental difference between Leibniz's perspectivism and Ortega's. While Leibniz's doctrine was couched in a monadological realism, Ortega's doctrine is embedded rather in a pluralistic realism. Thus Ortega proclaims the fact that strict coincidence of two views of reality would yield a pure abstraction, unless it were the outcome of an hallucination. Two views on the same reality cannot be strictly coincident, but at most complementary. This does not mean that complementary views are easy to obtain even if, following Ortega's recommendations, the individual tries to avoid distortion by faithfully reproducing his own perspective[2]. Confronted with Ortega's optimism on this issue, the reader may retort by

[1] I, 321 (1914).
[2] II, 18–20 (1916).

simply pointing out the strenuous and unsucessful attempts made by contemporary philosophers to solve the problem of the so-called intersubjectivity of individual statements. He may recall that schools of philosophy differing as widely among themselves as Husserlian phenomenologists and logical positivists have been compelled to slice off extensive fragments of their theories because of their failure to avoid solipsism after upholding a certain type of perspectivism. To such objections it is probable that Ortega would remain unyielding. He would certainly argue that his own brand of perspectivism is free from these drawbacks, precisely because he had previously got rid of subjectivistic or idealistic assumptions. He would, in short, claim that perspective is never a merely 'subjective' affair but an element or constituent of reality itself. Had Ortega used in this connection a more technical vocabulary, he might have stated that the term 'perspectivistic' is both an ontological and a psychological predicate. Perspectives, in other words, are the concrete sides of reality as perceived by concrete beings.

Ortega's theory of perspectives received both a confirmation and a clarification in 1923 in his *The Modern Theme*. As his first written attempt to present his arguments in a cogent way, this new exposition of perspectivism is particularly noteworthy. Perspectivism is now no longer an incidental remark or a mere project to be carried out when time permits. It is the corner-stone of a philosophical discipline: theory of knowledge. Leaning upon certain results of contemporary biology and psychology, Ortega assumes as a matter of fact that the reality denoted by the term 'subject' is, so to speak, an epistemological 'medium'. This medium of knowledge is, however, neither purely active nor entirely passive; namely it is neither a distorting nor a transparent vehicle of outside impressions. It may be compared to a selective screen, indefatigably engaged in sifting out what philosophers call 'the given'. Hence the possibility of considering each knowing subject as a private and yet faithful mirror of reality, barring of course conscious and deliberate distortion. That Ortega's analysis in this respect is couched in biological language is a fact that some commentators on his thought have not failed to notice and even to censure. Such comments seem to be all the more plausible as Ortega has often shown a predilection for biological science, in particular of the von Uexküll-Driesch brand. He has even seemed prone to consider 'life' from the point of view of biological impulse, thus sharing the well-known biologistic tendencies of such philosophers as Nietzsche or Simmel, not to speak of the numerous attempts at reducing knowledge to a process guided by biological utility. These interpretations have, in short, denounced Ortega's philosophy as biologically oriented. This, of course would not be in the least vexatious for a positivistic-minded philosopher, one who would dismiss as meaningless talk not only Heidegger's contempt for a merely 'ontical' view of life but also Dilthey's conception of life as a historical reality. Ortega, however, is not a positivistic-minded philosopher and consequently he has been rather touchy on this issue. Various reasons may be adduced in his defence. Let us mention three of them.

The first of these is based upon Ortega's idea that statements *in modo obliquo* cannot be avoided by a philosopher. Among such statements we may count, on the one hand, comparisons, and on the other hand, metaphors. It might then very well be the case that Ortega's biological language was either comparative or metaphorical. The second one is derived from the need of meeting the requirements of polemics. Faced with the question of how to lay sufficient stress on life against the encroachments of pure reason, the philosopher might have imagined that biological language would give more cogency to his arguments than the usual ontological or epistemological vocabulary. As the third reason, we may again point out that since perspectives belong both to the subject and to the object they cannot be reduced to a mere biological sifting of impressions. We do not know which reason Ortega would prefer. It is beyond doubt, however, that he would not accept a biological interpretation of knowledge, however difficult it proves to lay down a theory of knowledge free from biological commitments without redeeming it at the same time from a biological terminology. He would argue that, after all, he had soon coupled the notion of the 'vital' with historical perspective, to such an extent that the word 'life' in a sentence like 'Each life is a point of view directed upon the universe'[1] denotes not only, or exclusively, a human individual but also a national community or a historical period. Here we have, be it said in passing, a theme that will grow bigger in Ortega's thought: historicism. This we shall discuss in our next section; for the time being let us conclude by saying that in Ortega's opinion perspectivistic truth, although partial, is none the less absolute. It fails only to be complete. But completeness, in the nonformal sense of this word, can only be attained, according to the Spanish philosopher, if we are willing to sacrifice a real point of view to a fictitious one[2].

[1] III, 200 (1923) [*The Modern Theme*, from now on cited as *Theme*, p. 91].
[2] III, 199 (1923) [*Theme*, p. 89].

32

Reality, as given to concrete human life and not as perceived by an abstract being, located nowhere, is thus one of the main tenets of Ortega's philosophy, at least during the period we are now discussing. He seems to be eager above all to show that the complaints of both rationalists and supernaturalists against the transient character of life and reality are nothing but phraseology and insincerity[1]. Reality and life are not supposed to stay for ever: their value and gracefulness are enhanced rather than diminished by their ever-changing nature. They are, in short, temporal, and only those who prefer to substitute shallow abstractions for them will attempt to deny what is not a theory but the most simple and evident of all facts. The passages in which Ortega keeps insisting upon the fact that reality and life are *both* valuable and perishable—or rather valuable because perishable—are too numerous to be quoted here[2]. Let us simply sum up his views on the subject by stating that he tries again and again to lay stress on mutability as opposed to fixity, on playful behaviour as opposed to utilitarian action, on richness of appetites against puritan restraint, and, last but not least, on acceptance of reality as opposed to reverence for utopia. The pleasures of life are ephemeral. So much the better; they are thus authentic. Spontaneity ruins conventions. No matter; it will give rise to new and better ones. Play seems to lack dignity. It is because we forget that pure science, art and philosophy are products of purely disinterested behaviour. The philosopher must therefore foster all that is living and real, namely all that is authentic. Echoing Nietzsche, Bergson and Simmel, Ortega seems now to overpraise the values of life and, in particular, of human life.

It would be too hasty, nevertheless, to reach such a conclusion. True, we often miss in Ortega's writings of this period, in spite of the undeniable plasticity and incisiveness of his style, the sharp-cut outlines that should be the rule among philosophers. As we have already pointed out, he makes so much of life at a bare biological level that we often find it difficult not to take his statements in this respect at their face value. A case in point is his flat assertion that 'pure biology must be given preference to ethics when judging the values of vitality'[3]. Another case in point is his contention that culture consists in certain biological activities 'neither more nor less biological than digestion or

---

[1] On sincerity see II, 481–90 (probably 1924) and IV, 513–6 (1924).
[2] See, for instance: II, 232–3 (1919); II, 283, 290–1, 293, 302 (1920); III, 141–242 (1923) [*Theme, passim*].
[3] II, 293 (1920).

33

locomotion'[1]. All this seems to be perfectly clear. But a number of passages may also be quoted that suggest a far less biologistic and, for that matter, vitalistic orientation. They show that life must not be understood in the classical sense of a substance, that is to say, as something existing by itself and being conceived only by itself. Life is not subsistent. It is not independent. In a quite significant passage Ortega writes that his fondness for the spontaneity and authenticity of life has nothing to do with Rousseaunian primitivism. Attention must be paid to the spontaneous and primitive life of the spirit 'in order to secure and enrich culture and civilization'[2]. The so-called spontaneous life would be of little value if it consisted in pure savagery or rusticity. Quite the contrary: the value of life must be measured by its capacity to create the values of culture. A reason for this is that life—and in particular human life—is always 'life with', with something or with somebody. Life exists in an 'environment', a word that has, of course, biological connotations but also sociological and even ontological ones. In another passage the philosopher writes that the biological notion of life is only a segment of a much broader concept and therefore cannot be reduced to its somatic meaning[3]. We are thus left in doubt about a concept that plays a fundamental rôle in Ortega's philosophy. Fortunately enough, such a doubt does not last. Vitalism, to be sure, remains as one important side of Ortega's thought, but as one side only. That this is the case we can see quite clearly in the more systematic presentation of Ortega's views contained in the book to which we have been referring, but which needs closer scrutiny: *The Modern Theme.*

The title itself, later considered by Ortega as being 'too solemn'[4], suggests to the reader the main aims of the author. Roughly speaking, the point is this. Modern philosophers, at least since the time of Descartes, have shown a strong propensity to rely almost entirely upon abstract universal truths. This propensity has been given a name: rationalism. According to it, man is supposed to be primarily a rational animal whose task consists in unearthing flawless, rational principles capable of working to perfection not only in the fields of philosophy and science but also in the fields of ethics and politics. From this

[1] III, 166–7 (1923) [*Theme*, p. 41].
[2] II, 283 (1920). See also III, 179 (1923) [*Theme*, p. 60].
[3] III, 164, note (1923) [not included in *Theme*, p. 38]; III, 189 (1923) [*Theme*, p. 74]. A *mise au point* in VI, 348 (1932) and in part in III, 270–80 (1924).
[4] IV, 404 (1932).

34

some momentous consequences ensue: the mistrust of human spontaneity, the propensity to utopian thought and, last but not least, the growing tendency to superimpose culture on life and pure reason on spontaneous behaviour. The reader may judge that this picture is oversimplified. As a matter of fact, it is. It may be reasonably doubted that the modern age, even if considered only in the works of the scientists and philosophers, is explicable solely in terms of rationalism. Ortega is not unaware of this difficulty. Accordingly he brings in another modern position, one running counter to the above. This position consists chiefly in the denial of universal truths and in the assertion of the mutability of life. It too has been given a name: relativism. Many modern empiricists and sceptics may be counted among its followers. Now as we have seen, neither rationalism nor relativism is in a position to cope with the difficulties raised by the factual coexistence of individual or historical perspective and the undeniable yearning for universal truth. The theme of our time amounts thus to the quest for a settlement of the dispute between rationalism and relativism. This statement is in tune with former views held by Ortega, who in 1916 had already declared that he felt no longer compelled to bear the label of 'modern man', because he wanted to be a 'twentieth century man'[1]. By this he implied that 'the modern theme' was already exhausted and the twentieth century marked the beginning of a new age facing new problems and striving for new solutions in philosophy, in science, in art, and in politics[2]. Thus the book is not merely written in opposition to the theme of the 'modern age' but in an effort to overcome it.

Against the alternative of pure reason or pure vitality a new doctrine is set forth according to which reason emerges from life while at the same time life cannot subsist without reason. Ortega takes this stand especially in relation to the much discussed clash between life and culture. He engages, of course, in a bitter struggle against all rationalistic tendencies to overpopulate the world with abstract principles. He asserts that principles must not be deprived of their vital basis; otherwise they would become, as Bradley wrote of Hegel's metaphysics, 'a bloodless ballet of categories'. He emphatically proclaims that overemphasis on 'culture', 'spiritual life' and the like is most of the time the result

[1] II, 22–4 (1916). This incidentally makes the English translation of Ortega's title *El tema de nuestro tiempo* as *The Modern Theme* somewhat misleading. An exact rendering whould be *The Theme of Our Time*.
[2] See VI, 304 (1922); 306 (1922) and 312 (1923).

35

of an ostrich-like, indeed a pharisaical attitude. We must therefore adopt a radically sincere attitude toward the requirements
of life. We must acknowledge that at least in its first stage the
emergence of human culture and hence of values and principles
is, to use Toynbee's terminology, a response to the challenge of
human life by its physical and historical environment. Cultural
values have, in short, their immediate origin in the *vital* needs
of the human individual. Once this is conceded, however,
another no less undeniable fact must be admitted. Cultural
values as vital functions are ultimately subjective facts. But these
facts obey objective laws. Pure vital functions, as, for instance,
the biological ones, are so to speak immanent in the biological
organism. Cultural functions, on the other hand, are transcendent or, as Ortega puts it, 'transvital'. It will be said perhaps
that such an idea is anything but novel, yet there is a sense in
which Ortega's conceptions may be said to differ from those of
his predecessors. It is a fact that, contrary to many, the Spanish
philosopher would never agree to the theory that there is a
break of continuity between pure vital functions and objective
laws governing cultural values. Hence his assertion that *all* cultural values are *also* subject to the laws of life[1]. The word 'life' has
therefore a very broad meaning, certainly not only a biological
meaning. As a matter of fact, it has a double meaning: a biological and a spiritual one[2]. These two meanings appear often
as mutually exclusive. Moral values are sometimes incompatible
with the pleasures of life. The recognition of aesthetic values
is not always accompanied by delight. But on neither side are we
permitted to conclude that each time the biological side exercises
its rights spiritual claims must be withdrawn and vice versa.
Although extreme separate poles, they belong to the same world
and they often counterbalance each other. In other words, men
willing to lend their ears to the 'modern theme' must not be
caught in the trap either of primeval vitality or of sophisticated
civilization.

True enough, Ortega insists at this stage more upon life and
its values—sincerity, impetuosity, pleasure—than upon culture
and its values—truth, goodness, beauty. He does this because he
believes that modern civilization has overemphasized the latter.
As a matter of fact, such overemphasis is not limited to the

[1] III, 169 (1923) [*Theme*, pp. 45–6].
[2] It should be noted that the meaning of the word 'spiritual' in Spanish
does not strictly coincide with its meaning in English. In Ortega's
works 'spiritual' is usually a designation for the realm of values as well
as for objective scientific laws.

modern epoch but has been a striking characteristic of the whole of Western civilization. The predominance of life still prevailed in the beginnings of Greek culture and civilization; but Western man from the time of Socrates has tried to enforce the laws of reason. Vital spontaneity has been curbed to such an extent that at the end of this long historical process it has been assumed that reason, namely pure reason, was the real substance of the universe[1]. Instead of viewing reason as 'a tiny island afloat on the sea of primeval vitality'[2], philosophers considered it the sea itself. They made a mistake, but it was, so to speak, a necessary mistake. If they had not tried to oust life from the realm of reason, life would never have crossed the boundaries of pure biological spontaneity. But they obviously went too far in that direction, and with the ousting of life came the ousting of reality. Pure reason finally conquered a whole kingdom, but it proved to be a kingdom without subjects. In view of this, a rediscovery of the potentialities of life remains imperative. But this rediscovery must not be a simple counter-clock-wise movement. Pure reason or thinking *more geometrico* is 'an acquisition we can never forgo'[3]. What remains to be done is to put it back in its place. Therefore, neither Rousseaunian primitivism nor romantic irrationalism can be accepted as healthy corrective measures. Thus the problem is how to pass a fair judgment on life. But before pronouncing sentence on the place of life in the whole of reality it is necessary to liberate it from its subservience to pure reason. In other words, we must recognize that 'reason is merely a form and function of life'[4]. Only then will a new type, *vital reason*, emerge.

With this new concept we are in a position to keep our former promise: to describe the third phase of Ortega's intellectual career by means of a formal presentation of his philosophy.

---

[1] III, 176–7 (1923) [*Theme*, pp. 55–6]. Also III, 540–3 (1927).
[2] III, 177 (1923) [*Theme*, p. 57].
[3] III, 178 (1923) [*Theme*, p. 58].
[4] *loc. cit.*

IV

Ratio-Vitalism

(a) The concept of vital reason

Although outlined in *The Modern Theme*, the concept of vital reason was badly in need of further clarification. As we have seen, Ortega's emphasis on life had led some critics to interpret his philosophy as a purely vitalistic, indeed biologistic philosophy. It has also been pointed out that such an interpretation, although it may be justified by the philosopher's tendency to use biological language, does not accord with some of his most notable statements. A year after the publication of *The Modern Theme* Ortega issued an article in his *Revista de Occidente* in which he expressed his opinion on that delicate subject. The article, characteristically entitled 'Neither Vitalism nor Rationalism'[1], made it perfectly plain that both philosophical tendencies were, in the author's opinion, entirely outmoded. Rationalism was to be rejected because it confused the use of reason with its abuse. As for vitalism, the very ambiguity of its meaning made it hardly acceptable to a philosopher. To begin with, two brands of vitalism can be singled out for distinction: biological vitalism and philosophical vitalism. The former is the name of a specific scientific theory and is, accordingly, of little help for the present purpose. The latter is the name of a method of knowledge and must be carefully scrutinized.

Now the expression 'philosophical vitalism' is again highly ambiguous. On the one hand, it claims to be a doctrine (defended among others, by pragmatists and empirio-criticists) according to which reason is a biological process governed by biological laws: the struggle for life, the law of economy, the principle of the least action. On the other hand, it purports to be a theory (chiefly worked out by Bergsonians) according to which reason is epistemologically helpless and must give way to an intuitive insight which only 'life' is capable of affording. In this last sense, vitalism is a method of knowledge sharply opposed to the rational method. Finally, it claims to be a philosophy asserting that knowledge is, and must necessarily be, of a rational character, except for the fact that as life remains the central philosophical issue, reason must try above all to probe its significance. Only this third brand of philosophical vitalism is accepted by Ortega as a fair description of his own philosophical position.

[1] III, 270–80 (1924).

38

It will be seen that the very meaning of the term 'vitalism' has been considerably watered down. This is, incidentally, one of the reasons why other less controversial and more descriptive labels are preferable, such as the doctrine of vital reason, the doctrine of historical reason, the doctrine of living reason[1] and, of course, ratio-vitalism. However, all have a common aim: to show that if philosophy is 'philosophy of life', this expression cannot be understood in exactly the sense given to it by some other philosophers: Simmel, Spengler, Bergson or Dilthey. True, Ortega does not consider his own philosophizing as strictly running counter to the Bergsonian and still less to the Diltheyan. But he has often implied that his 'philosophy of vital reason' lies on a more advanced level both in time and in philosophical acuteness than the plain 'philosophy of life' of his predecessors. The mistrust of reason pervading all of them is no longer held by the Spanish philosopher as a necessary condition for acknowledging the central place of life in a philosophical system. In Ortega's opinion, such a mistrust is due to the fact that the term 'reason' was invariably identified by these philosophers with the expressions 'pure reason', 'abstract reason' and 'physical reason' (we may add 'mathematical reason' and 'physico-mathematical reason'). The failure of pure reason to understand life was, of course, a sound warning that such a reason was in need of strong criticism[2]. But the collapse of pure reason is not the collapse of *all* reason. It would therefore be a mistake to suppose that the failure of traditional rationalism leaves the way clear for plain irrationalism. As a matter of fact, irrationalism, so unfortunately welcomed in certain contemporary philosophical circles, is no less dangerous—and is far more helpless—than rationalism. Once more, then, rationalism and irrationalism are the result of a blindness to two equally significant sides of reality. Rationalism in particular has been guilty of sterilizing reason 'by amputating or devitalizing its decisive dimension'[3], by forgetting that reason 'is every such act of the intellect as brings us into contact with reality'[4]. Thus a new type of reason emerges, but, it must

[1] The expressions 'vital reason' and 'historical reason' are very often found in Ortega's writings from 1924 on. For 'living reason' see V, 135 (1935). For 'ratio-vitalism' see VI, 196 note (1934) [*Concord*, p. 184]. It should be noted that *razón vital* (vital reason) appears translated also as 'living reason' in *Concord*, *loc. cit.*
[2] VI, 23 (1936) [*Toward a Philosophy of History*, from here on cited as *Toward*, p. 183].
[3] VI, 46 (1936) [*Toward*, p. 226].
[4] *loc. cit.*

be noted, this type of reason is not a new *theory* about reason but the plain recognition of the *fact* that, whatever man thinks of reason, it is always rooted in his life.

Vital reason appears therefore to Ortega as a reality—a simple, unassailable, self-evident reality. As a matter of fact, the expression 'vital reason' is tantamount to the expression 'life *as* reason'. For it is assumed that life—by which we shall henceforth understand human life—is not an entity *endowed with* reason but rather an entity that *necessarily uses* reason even when it seems to behave unreasonably. No matter how thoughtlessly a man acts, in some way or other he will always account for what he does. The way he does it is quite immaterial. He may repent of behaving as he does, or he may claim that man is a strange sort of animal, loving the good and yet bowing down to evil. At any rate, life cannot exist without tirelessly accounting for itself. Now since to live is, as Ortega would put it, to contend with the world[1], human life must also account for the world that surrounds it. Let us add, however, that this process of 'accounting for' is not exclusively of an intellectual nature. Intellectual explanations of oneself and of the world are, indeed, latecomers in the process of human living. Ortega keeps repeating that life is impossible without knowledge, because knowledge is, above all, *knowledge of how to act*—a rather clumsy translation of Ortega's definition: *saber es saber a qué atenerse*[2]. In other words, man can live as he pleases, but he cannot live without doing his utmost to dispel the mist of doubts ever surrounding him. In fact, reason was, as it were, invented by man in order to counteract his tendency to cast doubts on everything, and in particular on himself[3]. Reason becomes thus the only possibility offered to man in order to help him carry on his own existence on the slippery ground of his life. Man is *not* therefore a rational animal, if this definition is understood in the sense that being an animal is the *genus proximum* and being rational the *differentia specifica*. But he *is* a rational animal if this definition is understood in the sense that reason emerges from human life. Descartes' principle *Cogito ergo sum* ('I think, therefore I am') must be replaced by a more basic principle: *Cogito quia vivo* ('I think, because I live')[4].

Although, as has been observed, vital reason is a reality, it is

---

[1] IV, 58 (1929); VI, 16 (1936) [*Toward*, p. 170]; V, 384 (1934).
[2] V, 85 (1933).
[3] IV, 108 (1930); V, 307-8 (1939); V, 530 (1941) [*Concord*, p. 64].
[4] IV, 58 (1929).

also a method[1]. Unfortunately, this method cannot be based upon a set of simple rules. As an outcome of life itself, vital reason as a method must follow the windings and meanderings of life. In a very radical sense of the word 'empirical', the method of vital reason is an empirical method. Now 'empirical' does not necessarily mean 'chaotic'. Idealist philosophers have assumed that the world is a chaos of impressions upon which a certain order is imposed by means of the so-called categories. To Ortega this is a completely gratuitous supposition. Experience shows rather that as soon as we bring life back to the center of philosophical inquiry, the world reveals itself as a well-ordered, a 'systematic' reality. Vital reason is thus no luxury for us. It is our guiding principle in our search for the 'system' of being. Faced with the problem of our own life, we cannot fail to throw upon it the light of understanding. The fact that most of the time such an understanding is vague or distorted or gathered from the beliefs treasured up by society is not an argument against its absolute necessity. Man's search for security is precisely one of the most powerful reasons for acknowledging the insecurity of his living. And as the best tool man has ever produced to cope with such a feeling of insecurity is reason, it will be now less hard to accept, and less difficult to understand, Ortega's repeated assertion that reason must always be conceived as something functional in human existence[2]. Again, thought is not something that man possesses and accordingly uses[3], but something that he painstakingly brings to existence because he needs it[4].

Stumbling through his own life and through the world into which he has been thrown, man is compelled to brood over his own situation, that is, to think about his circumstances. But to think about circumstances is really to think *in view of* circumstances. Therefore, the attempt to discover what we are and what are our surroundings is not a task exclusively incumbent upon the 'intellectual'—the philosopher, the scientist, the artist; it is a burden we shoulder for the mere fact of living[5]. Man *needs* to know himself and his circumstances. He needs, accordingly, an idea or an 'interpretation' of the world. This is, in Ortega's opinion, the primary sense of the expression 'Man must have his own convictions'. For what is called 'a man without con-

[1] Julián Marías, *op. cit.* and *Introducción a la filosofía*, Madrid: Revista de Occidente, 1947, pp. 205–16.
[2] VI, 351 (1932); VI, 391 (1942) [*Concord*, p. 199].
[3] IV, 108 (1930).
[4] IV, 108 (1930); V, 307–8 (1933-39).
[5] V, 88 (1933).

victions' is a non-existent entity[1]. These convictions may be of a negative character. A given individual may be, for example, a sceptic. It is none the less true that negative convictions are still convictions. Ortega has clarified this important point in many of his writings. One of them, however, is particularly enlightening for our purpose. It is the essay entitled 'Ideas and Beliefs' ('Ideas y creencias') which purported to be the first chapter of a systematic book on historical reason—and hence, as we shall see later, vital reason[2]. A brief description of its content will help us to understand the meaning of vital reason both as a method and as a reality.

In the first place, it is necessary to introduce a distinction. Hitherto we have referred indiscriminately to 'reason', to 'ideas', to 'convictions', but the term 'idea' may be understood at least in two senses. On the one hand, ideas are thoughts which *occur* to us or to somebody else and which we can examine, adopt or even parrot. These thoughts have a varying degree of truth. They may be ordinary thoughts or very rigorous scientific statements. In both cases, thoughts arise from within a human life existing before them. On the other hand, ideas are interpretations of the world and of ourselves which do not arise from within our existence but are, so to speak, an essential part of this existence. If the former ideas may be called, after all, *ideas*, we need another name for the latter ones. Ortega calls them *beliefs*. Contrary to ideas *simpliciter*, we do not arrive at beliefs by specific acts of thinking. As a matter of fact, we do not *arrive at* them at all. They are already in us, making up the substance of our life. In us? In fact, inasmuch as we coexist with our beliefs we can also be said *to be* in them. Consequently, beliefs are not ideas that we hold but rather ideas that we are. So deep-rooted are beliefs that we confuse them with reality and we find it difficult to disentangle our beliefs about reality from reality itself.

Thus the difference between ideas and beliefs is tantamount to the difference between thoughts which we produce, examine, discuss, disseminate, accept, deny or formulate, and thoughts which we do not formulate, discuss, deny or accept. As Ortega says, we really *do* nothing with beliefs; we *are* simply *in* them. It will be easily seen that the distinction between ideas and beliefs is not of a psychological nature and has scarcely to do with degrees of psychological certainty. Evidence, for instance, does

[1] V, 70 (1933).
[2] V, 381–409 (1934). Also: V, 87 (1933); VI, 11 (1936) [*Toward*, p. 174]; VI, 61 (1940) [*Concord*, pp. 18–9].

not make up a belief. It is rather the result of mental acceptance and, as such, can only be predicated of ideas. The point of view of psychology, although highly respectable, is insufficient for tackling this problem. Another less specialized point of view must be taken, 'the point of view of life'. In short, a thought is called an idea *or* a belief according to the rôle it plays in human existence. The contrast between ideas and beliefs boils down, therefore, to the contrast between thinking about a thing and taking it for granted. 'To be in a belief' is, in fact, the same thing as to take an idea for granted. Here lies, be it said in passing, the reason why it would be a gross misunderstanding simply to identify beliefs with religious beliefs. Religious beliefs, it is true, often do deserve this name, but this is not necessarily so, because we frequently call religious beliefs what are in many cases nothing but plain ideas. On the other hand, many simple and elementary assumptions may be called beliefs. We believe, for instance, when deciding to go out into the street, that there is a street, even if the thought of the existence of a street has not entered our minds and seems to play no rôle in our decision. We believe that there is a certain regularity in natural phenomena in exactly the same sense as certain people have formerly believed that there was no regularity in natural phenomena. Examples could be multiplied. All of them, however, would converge on the same characteristic of a latent, non-formulated and sometimes even non-formulable thought we take continually for granted and which sustains, impels and directs our behaviour. No wonder beliefs form the foundation of our life and take the place of reality. Reality is not discovered by us. Nor is it proven by us. It is simply something we come up against. This means that to a certain extent we dominate our ideas, but are, in return, dominated by our beliefs. However important ideas may prove to be for us, they cannot take root in our life unless they cease to be ideas and become beliefs. This is why it is hard to accept the usual intellectualist interpretation of ideas. Intellectualists are incapable of understanding that ideas are external to us, that we can take or leave them at random. They are even incapable of understanding that on some occasions the reality upon which they place the highest value—reason—*may* become an authentic belief and accordingly escape criticism and examination. But perhaps the most striking difference between ideas and beliefs is that which Ortega has pointed out at the very beginning of his essay on this subject: while we can set so high a value on ideas that we are willing to fight and even to die *for* them, it is utterly impossible to live *on* them.

The reader may find that, no matter how plausible all this may seem, Ortega's arguments are not flawless. A moment ago we suggested that, according to the Spanish philosopher, man is unceasingly casting doubts upon his own life or, in other words, that man's existence is deeply problematic. Furthermore, we shall discover that this is by no means an incidental remark, but a central issue in Ortega's philosophy of human existence. How are these assertions to be reconciled with the above scheme? Ortega is not unaware of this difficulty. And in order to avoid confusion he makes it plain that doubt is not something opposed to belief but is rather 'a kind of belief'. Two considerations may help to understand this paradoxical opinion. First, beliefs are never without gaps—and 'enormous gaps', indeed. Second, doubts—in the very radical sense of this word—are not simply upheld by us and, accordingly, are not ideas. Doubts belong, in short, to the same stratum of life as beliefs: the former make up our reality in a sense not altogether different from the latter. And this means, of course, that we *are in* doubts in exactly the same sense as we *are in* beliefs. The sole difference between them is that while beliefs are 'stable things' doubts are 'unstable things'. Doubts are, properly speaking, 'what is unstable' in human existence. But, of course, we live simultaneously with both of them, so that our existence would be as little thinkable without doubts as it is without beliefs.

The fact that we are *also* in doubts or even, as Ortega writes, 'in a sea of doubts', does not preclude, however, the fact that we accept this situation as a normal state of affairs. As a matter of fact, we are unceasingly doing our utmost to rise above the doubt undermining our existence. Now in order to free ourselves of doubts we have but one choice: to think about them or, what comes to the same thing, to bring forth ideas. Ideas are supposed to fill the gaps that open here and there in the beliefs that make up human life. This seems at the outset to be scarcely plausible if we scrutinize our experience, for experience teaches us that actions rather than ideas cut the Gordian knot of our doubts. But plausibility increases if we pay attention to the fact that, according to the Spanish philosopher, no clear-cut line is to be drawn between action and contemplation. Action, writes Ortega, is certainly governed by contemplation, but at the same time contemplation—adumbration of ideas—is in itself a project for action[1]. Ideas may thus be considered as our sole possibility of keeping afloat on the sea of doubts. And it is not in the least

[1] V, 304 (1933-39); VI, 391 (1942) [*Concord*, p. 99].

uncommon to replace our former beliefs, shaken to the roots, by new ideas—which have a tendency to become beliefs. This can be experienced in our personal life. But there is a field in which the substitutions referred to are revealed with the utmost clarity: human history. Many of Ortega's examples are drawn from historical experience. To Ortega's reader this will not come as a surprise. Our writer has always been a true lover of history. Some of his finest essays are devoted to historical problems. He has, besides, often claimed that one of the outstanding characteristics of contemporary Western society is the full development of a feeling that had already been foreshadowed in the eighteenth century: the feeling that man is not an immutable creature living in a historical setting but an entity whose reality is decisively shaped by his own history. We shall call this feeling 'historical sense'. Since 1924, Ortega has made many remarks on this issue[1]. He has even been led to acknowledge that history is not only the subject-matter of a science but the ultimate condition of human existence. We shall later examine Ortega's assertion that man has no nature but has instead history. At present we shall limit ourselves to pointing out that the interplay between beliefs and ideas on the one hand and between beliefs and doubts on the other hand is confirmed by the events of history. The theory of historical crises and the detailed analysis of some of these crises[2] has made it clear that human life starts from beliefs, that is to say, from convictions which lie deep in the historical environment. As these convictions are shaken every now and then, they must be replaced by others—including the conviction that no convictions are at present available. The most adequate tool for the understanding of this problem is the method of historical reason. Now, before bringing this matter to an issue, we cannot help but venture a few remarks on a question which appears to be purely verbal, but which has given Ortega's commentators some trouble: that of the relationship between historical reason and vital reason.

First of all, if man is a historical being it seems inescapable that vital reason is identical with historical reason. Ortega's occasional hesitations in the use of these expressions have led some interpreters to assert that he jumped from the first to the second as a

---

[1] III, 260–4 (1924); III, 245–54 (1924); III, 281–316 (1924); V, 495 (1940); VI, 385–8 (1942) [Concord, pp. 92–6].
[2] V, 9–164 (1933); V, 492–507 (1940). Also Invertebrate Spain, The Revolt of the Masses and, to a certain extent, The Dehumanization of Art.

consequence of the deep impression made upon him by Wilhelm Dilthey's philosophy[1]. In some respects this does seem to be the case. Nevertheless, there is no denying the fact that Ortega has been eager to include historical reason in vital reason by emphasizing at the same time their homonymity and their synonymity. Let us assume for a moment that it would have been more plausible to substitute 'historical epoch' for 'human life' and 'historical reason' for 'vital reason'. But the fact that human life is basically a historical entity can be interpreted in two ways. First, we can do it in an all-out manner. In this case, Ortega's philosophy of vital reason would emerge as a sample of pure historicism. Yet there is also a moderate way of interpreting it. Then Ortega's philosophy of vital reason may provide the metaphysical basis for all philosophies, including historicism. In other words, if the first interpretation of the doctrine is accepted, then vital reason will be at the mercy of the waves of history. If, on the other hand, the second interpretation is preferred, then the statement that man is a historical being will have to be diluted and lose many of its implications. Two solutions may be offered in order to overcome these difficulties. One is Julián Marías' contention that Ortega's notion of historical reason, unlike Dilthey's, is to be understood as an operation of life and history rather than as life and history themselves[2]. Another is Ortega's assumption that what we call the doctrine of vital reason is not, properly speaking, a doctrine, but the consequence of a plain fact: the fact that human life—which again is historical in character—is an entity that cannot escape using reason at large if it aspires to penetrate its own structure and significance. We cannot unfortunately elucidate this momentous question here. The analysis of human existence that follows will perhaps help the reader to make up his mind on this thorny subject.

(b) The doctrine of man

The doctrine of human life is a central issue—or rather *the* central issue—in Ortega's philosophy. Let us hasten to assure the reader that no idealism and, of course, no anthropocentrism are involved in this position. Human life is certainly not the sole reality in the universe. It can hardly be said to be the most

---

[1] See Eduardo Nicol, *Historicismo y existencialismo*, México: El Colegio de México, 1952, pp. 308–31. On Ortega's account of Dilthey see V, 165–214 (1933–34) [*Concord*, pp. 129–82].
[2] Julián Marías, *Introducción a la filosofía*, p. 212.

important reality. But it is, as Ortega puts it, the *basic* reality, since all the other realities appear within it[1].

The relationship between human life—namely, *each* human life—and the other realities must not be misunderstood. It would be a deplorable error to suppose that human life is a 'thing' within the frame of which other 'things' exist. Not being a thing, human life cannot be defined the way things usually are— by saying, for instance, that it has a certain nature, or that it is a substance or a law governing apparently unrelated phenomena. Human life—an expression synonymous with 'life', 'our life', 'human reality', 'man', etc.—is not reducible to our body, al- though, as we shall presently see, it cannot keep itself in existence without a body. To think otherwise is to contradict what has been said earlier about vital reason. In other words, it is tanta- mount to imagining that pure reason or physical reason sheds on human life that same vivid light it casts upon natural phenomena. Realism and naturalism, handy though they are in particular fields of knowledge like physics or biology, must be laid aside when the reality we face is the 'basic reality'. Shall we say then that our life is a soul, or a spirit, or a mind, or a consciousness? Idealists have, in fact, made this proposal. But idealism, or the philosophy of mind, is as useless for our purpose as realism, or the philosophy of things, or as naturalism, or the philosophy of matter. They are all the wrong type of philosophy or, to be more exact, the wrong type of ontology. After all, soul, mind, spirit, consciousness, thought and the like are to a certain extent things, as Descartes made clear in calling matter *res extensa* and thought *res cogitans*. In spite of the efforts of idealist philosophers to describe the reality of the ego without falling into the traps set by pure naturalism, they have always patterned their theories on the assumptions of traditional ontology. The same old mis- takes made by realists have again and again crept into their analyses of human existence, thus making it impossible to seize hold of its paradoxical structure.

Human life is, therefore, neither body nor mind, neither a thing like matter nor a thing like spirit. What is it then? Some philosophers, anxious to solve the riddle of the mind-body problem, have reached the conclusion that human life is a 'neu- tral' entity, which can be called mind *or* body, depending upon the viewpoint taken upon it. It would seem at first that there is no wide difference' between this opinion and Ortega's. If that were the case, Ortega's philosophy of human life would be quite

[1] V, 83, 95 (1933); V, 347 (1932); VI, 13, 32 (1936) [*Toward*, p. 165, p. 198]; VI, 347 (1932).

close to a 'neutralism' of Mach's or Russell's type. Confronted with this issue, the Spanish philosopher would, however, emphatically deny such 'neutralistic' leanings. He would at most admit that his doctrine of man coincides with that of the neutralists in what they deny, but not in what they assert. For neutralism uses also willy-nilly the same concepts of traditional ontology. Like idealists or realists, neutralists assume that the reality of human life follows the pattern of the ontology of 'things'. But again human life is not a thing. It is not even a 'being'. It has no fixed status; it has no nature. Life *happens* to each one of us. It is a pure 'happening' or, as Ortega puts it, a gerundive, a *faciendum*, and not a participle, a *factum*. Instead of being something ready-made, we have to make it unceasingly. Life, in short, is a 'being' that makes itself, or rather 'something' consisting in making itself. In consequence of it, the concept of becoming, which some philosophers have propounded as a substitute for the concept of being, is only a trifle more adequate than the latter for the description of human existence. True, Ortega's philosophy draws nearer to a 'metaphysics of becoming' than to any other type of philosophy. After all, he has written that 'the time has come for the seed sown by Heraclitus to bring forth its mighty harvest'[1] and he has agreed that Bergson, 'the least Eleatic of thinkers', was right in many points[2]. But Heraclitus' philosophy of becoming was a mere hint, and Bergson's conception of *l'être en se faisant* is marred by an irrationalistic metaphysics for which Ortega feels but little sympathy. Fichte was, in fact, closer to grasping the true being of life than any other philosopher and was even on the point of discovering its basic structure. But his persistent intellectualism compelled him to think in 'Eleatic fashion'. A new ontology is, therefore, needed —an ontology equally distrustful of intellectualism and irrationalism, and capable of getting rid of the Eleatic remains still dragged along by the so-called dynamic philosophies of becoming.

How is such an ontology to be created? The answer has already been given: by the method of vital reason. When pure rationalism has collapsed in its attempt to understand human life, and when irrationalism has dissolved into an affected pathos, life as reason comes to the rescue. It shows that practically everything that has been said on human life is nothing but a more or less gratuitous theory superimposed upon life. But human life, again, is no theory: it is a plain fact. Before proceeding to theorize

[1] VI, 34 (1936) [*Toward*, p. 203].
[2] *loc. cit.*

48

about human life, it will be wiser to give an account of it. Theory will thus emerge as a result of our description instead of being an *a priori* mental framework having only a very remote bearing on our 'basic reality'.

What does vital reason discover in its description of human life? To begin with, we have already indicated the negative features. Human life is, properly speaking, neither mind nor body. Mind and body are realities we have to live and contend with, in exactly the same sense as we have to live and contend with our physical and social environment. We find ourselves in a world which has not been chosen by us. We live in constant intercourse with our circumstances. We are not a 'thing' but *the* person *who* lives a *particular* and *concrete* life with things and among things. There is no abstract and generic living. Ortega's old principle, 'I am myself and my own circumstances', therefore plays a fundamental rôle in the descriptive ontology of human life. Against realists, Ortega claims, as we have seen, that our life is the basic reality and the point of departure for any sound philosophical system. Against idealists, he holds that life can only be understood as an entity fully immersed in the world. Ortega's statements in this respect are numerous. Life exists as 'a perpetual migration of the vital Ego in the direction of the Not-self'[1]. To live is 'to hold a dialogue with the environment'[2], namely, 'to deal with the world, to turn to it, to act on it'[3]. To live is to be outside oneself[4], to contend with something[5], with the world and with oneself. In short, to live is always *to live with*. For that reason, human life is not a 'subjective event'. It is the most objective of all realities. Now, among the realities we live and contend with, we must count our physiological mechanisms and our psychological dispositions. Helped by them or hindered by them, we must make our life and be faithful to our innermost *ego*, to our 'call', to our 'vocation'[6]. This 'vocation' is strictly individual. Not all the human destinies have the same degree of concreteness, but all personal 'vocations' are untransferable. What psychologists call 'character' is, in fact, only one among the many factors determining the course of our existence. It would be a gross mistake to suppose, therefore, that our life is

---

[1] III, 180 (1923) [*Theme*, p. 72].
[2] III, 291 (1924).
[3] III, 607 (1924) [*Toward*, p. 14].
[4] IV, 400, 426 (1932).
[5] V, 384 (1934).
[6] IV, 411 (1932); *Papeles sobre Velázquez y Goya*, Madrid: Revista de Occidente, 1951, pp. 68–9.

solely determined by the external environment or by our character. Schlegel's belief that our talents correspond to our tastes is, in Ortega's opinion, a grave misunderstanding. For if it is sometimes true that our tastes and our talents happily harmonize, it is unfortunately not unusual for them to clash violently. Let us suppose that you have a gift for mathematics. But what if you are irresistibly called to become a lyrical poet? Let us imagine that we are endowed with the talents of a merchant. But what if we secretly crave to become scholars? The above examples are, however, not sufficiently effective. Being a merchant or a lyrical poet is, after all, a way of life set up by society and, as such, cannot be compared to the 'call' that forms the very basis of our personal 'destiny'. The examples are effective though, in so far as they show that tastes and talents do not always go together and that the ensuing struggle between a man's personal destiny and his psychological character often accounts for the frequent feeling of frustration so characteristic of human existence. They are effective also in so far as they show that the world is not for us a collection of 'things' but rather a complex of 'situations'. Things—and ideas—are nothing but difficulties or facilities for existing[1]. We can even say that as books are made up of pages, human existence is made up of situations[2]. Thus man finds himself with a body, with a mind, with a psychological character, exactly as he finds himself, with capital left by his parents, with a country where he was born, with a historical tradition[3]. As we have to live with our liver, be it healthy or diseased, we have to live with our intelligence, be it bright or dull. However much we may complain about the weakness of our memory, we have to live with it and carry on our life *by means* of it. The life of a man is not, therefore, the operating of the mechanisms with which Providence has graced him. We must constantly ask in *whose* service these mechanisms operate. The question, in short, is not what I am but *who* I am.

Confronted with *all* these circumstances, man is forced to make his own life and to make it, whenever possible, in an authentic fashion[4]. This is, incidentally, the main reason why what we do in our life is *not* immaterial. In his essay on Goethe, Ortega has pointed out that Goethe's celebrated sentence, 'My actions are merely symbolic', was but a way of concealing from himself the

[1] VI, 32 (1936) [*Toward*, p. 200].
[2] V, 96 (1933).
[3] IV, 399 (1932).
[4] On the 'authentic *ego*' as the 'unbribable basis' of our life, see also II, 84–5 (1916).

decisive character of his behaviour. As a matter of fact, our actions are not symbolic; they are real. We cannot, therefore, act 'no matter how'. Human life has nothing to do with 'No matter', 'Never mind' or 'It is all one to me'. Neither can we act as we please. We have to act as we must act; we have to do what we have to do. It is unfortunate, of course, that upon reaching this deep stratum of our existence the only statements we seem capable of uttering are either tinged with morality or marred by triviality. 'To act as we must act' seems to be a moral rule—a kind of categorical imperative still more formal and far less normative than the Kantian one. It is nothing of the kind. It simply states that we must bow to our purely individual call, *even if it runs counter to the conventional rules of morality*[1]. It is possible, of course, to offer resistance to our destiny. But our life will be then less authentic and, to a certain extent, less real. 'To do what we have to do' seems a pure tautology. It is rather a way of enlightening us about the fact that our concrete actions, if they are to be real and not merely symbolic, must spring from the sources of our authentic, and often hidden, *ego,* and must not be diverted by any conventional rule, by any of the many temptations leading to the falsification of our existence. For human life can easily falsify itself and thus become less real. Nature does not admit of degrees of reality, but human existence does[2]. Therefore, 'what man does can be more or less authentic and hence more or less real'[3]. This does not mean, of course, that to be unauthentic and to be non-existent are exactly the same things. It means that human life possesses sometimes the 'defective mode' of reality which we call inauthenticity.

Every reader will agree that the above descriptions raise a number of questions. How do we know about our authentic *ego*? Would an authentic life be possible without a certain amount of falsification and hence of frustration? Why are moral rules of the so-called conventional kind to be so drastically discarded? The elucidation of any one of these questions would certainly fill an entire volume. Here it will be sufficient to say that whatever objections are raised, they will have to meet Ortega's assumptions on a common ground. This ground is not ethical but metaphysical—perhaps we should say, ontological. Only from a metaphysical point of view will the above assertions become meaningful. The same viewpoint must be taken when

[1] IV, 406 (1932).
[2] VI, 400 (1942) [*Concord,* p. 108, note].
[3] *loc. cit.*

interpreting such Ortegean apophthegm as 'Life is a problem', 'Life is a task', 'Life is a preoccupation with itself', 'Life is a shipwreck', and 'Life is a vital programme'.

'Life is a problem' is not a trivial, matter-of-fact statement. It does not simply mean that we are often beset by problems. After all, a number of people seem to get along surprisingly well with their troubles. It means that life *itself* is a trouble, a problem, or, to use Ortega's vocabulary, that human life is made up of the problem of itself[1]. Human life is accordingly a most serious business, certainly far more serious than art, science or philosophy. The so-called great problems amount to little when compared to the startling problem of our own life. Now life is a problem because it is a task, a problematical task. Again, we are not faced here with the tasks and toils of life but with *the* task and toil that human life itself *is*. Making use of a very plastic Spanish term, Ortega defines life as a *quehacer*—what *has* to be done[2]. But *what* has to be done? In principle, only this: our *own* life. Is this not an overwhelming, almost unbearable toil? To begin with, we cannot make our own lives as we make other things— houses, symphonies or philosophical systems. These things we make according to a delicate mixture of rules and inspirations. But there are no rules for the making of our lives. The sole rule we can lay down is: perpetual discovery of our being. We can thus say that our life is a *causa sui*, a cause of itself. But even this proves to be an understatement. In fact, human life has not only to cause itself; it has also to determine the self it is going to cause. We have *always* to decide what we are going to do with our lives. Not for a single moment is our activity of decision allowed to rest[3]. Here lies the reason why freedom is not something we are endowed with but something we really *are*. We are free beings in a most radical sense, because we feel ourselves *fatally* compelled to exercise our freedom[4]. Man is free by compulsion[5], for even when he forsakes his liberty he has to decide it beforehand. We must therefore commit ourselves perpetually, not because there is a moral rule stating that we have to, or because we happen to think that commitment is a nobler attitude than non-commitment, but because we cannot escape this inexorable condition of our existence. Freedom is so absolute in human life that we can

[1] IV, 403 (1932).
[2] IV, 366 (1932); IV, 414 (1932); V, 341 (1933-39) [*Toward*, p. 116]; VI, 13 (1936) [*Toward*, p. 165]; VI, 421 (1942).
[3] VI, 33 (1936) [*Toward*, p. 202].
[4] IV, 171 (1930) [*Revolt*, p. 52].
[5] *loc. cit.*

even chose not to be 'ourselves', namely, not to be faithful to that innermost self of ours which we have given above the name of personal destiny. Our freedom, however, will not decrease owing to the fact that our life becomes inauthentic, because freedom is precisely the absolute possibility of reaching or not reaching the inner 'call' sustaining our lives.

No wonder therefore that human life is always a preoccupation with itself. We are constantly worried by the diverse possibilities among which we have to choose. It is true that society helps us to decide in a great number of cases; otherwise, our life would become an unbearable burden. It is true also that circumstances, *in view of* which and *by means of* which we carry out our lives, are a most welcome guide in the course of our decisions. It is true, finally, that however 'plastic' our existence is, it is an irreversible process, so that the past—personal and collective past—shapes our present and produces more and more limitations to our future behaviour[1]. But ultimate decisions are always a purely personal affair. Inasmuch as solitude—'existential' and not merely 'physical' solitude—is an outstanding feature of human life, only decisions made in complete solitude will really be authentic[2]. Moreover, such decisions must always be made 'from the future'. Human life is also, therefore, a 'vital design', a 'vital programme'[3]—expressions which, to a certain extent, are synonymous with 'call', 'vocation' and 'destiny'. Again, to this design we may or we may not respond. For that very reason life exists in a constant state of uneasiness and insecurity. It has been said, incidentally, that this last statement conflicts with some other typically Ortegean opinions. Some critics, for example, have argued that you cannot define life as uneasiness if you have previously stated that sportive activity is the most serious and important part of life[4], or if you have asserted that it is necessary, whenever possible, to get rid of dullness and austerity and to steer instead a course for joy[5]. To such criticisms Ortega would probably retort that uneasiness is not incompatible with joyful vitality and that his definition of life as insecurity is old enough for him to wave aside any objections[6]. At all events, Ortega's metaphysics of human life implies insecurity as one of its out-

[1] VI, 37 (1936) [*Toward*, p. 208).
[2] V, 23 (1933).
[3] II, 645 (1929); IV, 77 (1930); IV, 400 (1932); V, 239 (1935).
[4] II, 350 (1924) [*Toward*, p. 18].
[5] *La redención de las provincias y la decencia nacional*, Madrid: Revista de Occidente, 1931, Chap. vii.
[6] I, 480 (1910).

standing features. The opinion that life is in itself a problem, the comparison of life with a shipwreck, are quite common in Ortega's works[1]. But insecurity is *not* everything in human existence. Together with man's perennial state of uneasiness, we must take into account his perpetual craving for security. What we usually call 'culture' is at bottom nothing but a life-boat which we launch and to which we cling in order to prevent us from sinking into the abyss of insecurity. Culture keeps us afloat[2]. This is, be it said in passing, one of the reasons why culture must *also* be authentic. We must prevent it from overloading itself with adipose tissue. We must do our utmost in order to reduce it to pure nerve and pure muscle. Otherwise we shall fall into a sin often exposed by Ortega: the bigotry of culture[3]. Culture is, in short, a possibility for liberation *or* for oppression. Whether it goes the one way or the other depends, of course, on its vitality, namely, on its authenticity[4]. Like human life, culture has to narrow itself down to the essential and throw off all that is non-essential.

Life is, therefore, task, problem, preoccupation, insecurity. It is also a drama[5]. For that very reason Ortega says that the primary and radical meaning of life is a biographical and not a biological one. We understand the meaning of life when we proceed to give a narrative of it, that is to say, when we try to describe the series of events and situations it has come up against and the vital design underlying them. Many reasons have been adduced to endorse the dramatic character of human existence. We shall add now another: the obvious fact that man is an ephemeral and transient being[6]. Man is always in a hurry. Life itself is haste and urgency. Pressed by time[7], man cannot cast about for excuses. He has to dash along in order to make the right decisions at the right time. He cannot wait. His life is precisely the opposite of the Greek calends[8]. He cannot form

[1] IV, 254 (1930) [*Revolt*, p. 170]; IV, 321 (1930) [*Mission of the University*, p. 56]; IV, 397, 412 (1932); V, 472 (1932); V, 24 (1933).
[2] I, 354-56 (1914); IV, 397 (1932).
[3] See specially *Theme*, *Revolt* and *Mission of the University*. Also V, 13-64, (1933) and V, 493-507 (1940).
[4] See, however, V, 78 (1933). Ortega seems to imply here that culture *always* ends by stifling the authentic life of the individual.
[5] IV, 77 (1930); IV, 194 (1940) [*Revolt*, p. 86]; IV, 400 (1932); V, 31, 37 (1933); V, 305 (1933-39); VI, 32 (1936) [*Toward*, p. 200]; *Papeles sobre Velázquez y Goya* (1950), p. 230.
[6] VI, 350 (1932).
[7] V, 37 (1933); VI, 421-22 (1942). *Papeles*, p. 58 (1950).
[8] VI, 22 (1936) [*Toward*, p. 182].

projects only to be carried out in an indeterminate future. He must strive urgently, hurriedly, for the main aim of his life: the 'liberation *toward* himself'[1]. He cannot simply let events do away with the estrangement that constantly threatens his existence with inauthenticity and falsification. Only after his liberation will he be able to discover what is perhaps the ultimate conclusion in his search for the basic reality: that it is useless to search for a transcendent reality, because what we call 'the transcendent' is life itself: man's own inalienable life[2]. Life is thus, as it were, *the* reality. This does not mean, again, that human life is the sole reality in the universe or even that it is a purely independent, incommunicable reality. After all, we have already emphasized that to live is 'to live with'—with the world, with other people, with society. But after due consideration we find that when man loses the beliefs that had nourished his existence, the only reality still left to him is his life, 'his disillusioned life'[3]. We seem thus driven to despair. But, in fact, only when we are ready to glance coldly and lucidly at this uncanny nature of our existence shall we become capable of holding our own ground and starting afresh our perpetual search after new forms and ways of living.

(c) The doctrine of society

Among the realities man lives with, society is a conspicuous one. Without prejudice to the individual's rights, there is no objection to saying that man is a social being. The analysis of society is accordingly a question of first importance.

From the beginning of his career, Ortega has acknowledged the exceptionally significant rôle played by social problems. Thoughts on the nature of society at large and on concrete societies, past or present, are frequent in his works. As a matter of fact, some of his most popular writings, like *Invertebrate Spain* and *The Revolt of the Masses*, are to a large extent analyses of social facts and problems. We do not therefore lay undue stress on this question by tackling it immediately after the problem of the 'basic reality'.

Ortega has grown into the habit of working out theories along with the study of concrete realities. His theory of society is no exception to the rule. Although he has often promised his

[1] IV, 425 (1932).
[2] IV, 540 (1928); IV, 56–59 (1929); IV, 70 (1930); IV, 345 (1932); V, 95 (1933); VI, 49 (1936) [*Toward*, p. 230].
[3] VI, 49 (1936) [*Toward*, p. 230].

readers a book on the individual and society, the book has not yet been published. Fortunately, there are in his works a number of significant pages, most of them translated into English[1], upon which we can entirely rely for a clear understanding of our subject. However, only the theory of society at large will be taken into consideration here. We take for granted that the reader is familiar with Ortega's most publicized views on social topics. In particular, his 'dissection of the mass-man', as contained in *The Revolt of the Masses*, has become a matter-of-course basis for contemporary discussions. The reader will probably remember that Ortega has forcefully criticized the mass-man—a type we can find on *all* levels of society—on account of his feelings of self-satisfaction, of his will to intervene in all matters and impose his own vulgar views, of his deplorable ignorance that 'nobility' is defined by the demands it makes on us rather than by the concessions or favours we enjoy. He will perhaps remember a little less sharply that Ortega has *also* acknowledged that the rule of the masses 'presents a favourable aspect, inasmuch as it signifies an all-round rise in the historical level, and reveals that average existence to-day moves on a higher plane than that of yesterday'[2]. Nevertheless, we shall have to drop this and other problems in order to attend to the most pressing thing: the nature of society as such.

'Society as such' is, incidentally, a misnomer. In fact, there is no 'society as such'. Society is a concrete, living reality which, like the individual, has no fixed nature but only a history. It is accordingly difficult fully to account for the 'nature' of society without paying attention to particular societies and to their historical development. Society, like man, is, according to Ortega, an entity impervious to pure, abstract reason. Its being can only be disclosed by means of vital, that is, narrative and historical, reason. From this point of view Ortega has examined diverse societies, in particular the old Roman society and the modern European one. Yet the examination of particular societies leads us sooner or later to an understanding of their common characteristics. In other words, knowledge about society can be conceptualized. The sole condition imposed on the concepts thus obtained is that they be, as Ortega puts it, 'occasional concepts', namely, concepts having only 'a formal identity that serves precisely to guarantee the constitutive nonidentity of the matter signified'[3].

[1] Besides the two books mentioned above, *Concord and Liberty*, pp. 11–47, is especially to be recommended.
[2] IV, 156 (1930) [*Revolt*, p. 31].
[3] VI, 35 (1936) [*Toward*, pp. 205–6].

On the above basis we can lay down a set of fundamental notions. The first we have already pointed out: as man exists in a physical world, he exists in a social world. Society is thus an 'element' where man 'moves and is'. The physical and the social world have something in common: they bring pressure to bear on our lives. The fact that social pressures are for the most part invisible, consisting as they do in uses, customs, rules, etc.[1], does not mean that they are less burdensome to us. We are accustomed to think of social pressure when this is brought to bear on us in a direct, physical way, as happens when we feel the pressure of the institutions of the State. But the State, says Ortega, is only *one* of the pressures of society, although it is the strongest one. The State is 'the superlative of society'[2]. Now, social pressure is not always unwelcome. It would be preposterous to think of society as Kant's dove 'thought' of the air: that without it we could enjoy much better our freedom of movement. Society does, in fact, a great deal to keep us afloat amidst our constant worries. It is a complex system of reciprocal actions—in particular, adds Ortega, of reciprocal actions between masses and minorities[3]— and, therefore, of reciprocal helps. Thus we need the social 'element' where we live lest we want to do everything by ourselves. A considerable fragment of our individual being is accordingly made up of social realities, namely, of social uses and customs[4]. At the same time that they stifle and oppress us, they prevent us from drowning. This is obvious even in the case of the strongest of all social pressures: the State. The State is not everything in society; it is only a part of society[5]. To deify it, as Hegel did, is 'a senseless mysticism'[6]. But even the State is inescapable. Our only hope lies in the possibility of living in an epoch when the State envelops the social body as elastically as the skin covers the organic body[7]. This happens when the history of society is 'in the ascendant', when people can shape the State after their vital preferences instead of adapting themselves to the iron mould of the State. In other words, when the State works like a skin, we have 'life in freedom'; when it works like an orthopaedic appara-

---

[1] VI, 38, 43 (1936) [*Toward*, pp. 210, 220]; V, 487 (1936); IV, 297 (1937); V, 296 (1939); VI, 53 (1940); VI, 88 (1940) [*Concord*, p. 33].
[2] V, 219 (1935); VI, 88 (1940) [*Concord*, p. 33]; VI, 397 (1942) [*Concord*, p. 105].
[3] III, 103 (1922).
[4] V, 485-7 (1936).
[5] IV, 295 (1937).
[6] IV, 221-8 (1930) [*Revolt*, pp. 127-136].
[7] VI, 83-107 (1940) [*Concord*, pp. 32-47].

tus, we have 'life as adaptation'. The State thus plays a dual rôle. This also happens with society. The concept 'society' proves, therefore, to be an 'occasional concept', with its meaning depending upon particular societies in particular epochs, although preserving always a certain degree of identity.

Society is thus both beneficial and harmful. It is like the air we breathe and also like a stumbling-block we encounter. This seems to wave aside all possible objections and dispense with further analysis. Unfortunately, the problem is somewhat more complex. To begin with, we find Ortega's description of the simultaneously beneficial and harmful character of society somewhat puzzling. On the one hand, society is necessary for us to the degree that we cannot conceive of ourselves unless welded to it. And this is not, of course, because we start with an *a priori* definition of man as a 'social being' or because we discover in our everyday life and in historical records an overwhelming empirical confirmation of the sociability of the human person. In Ortega's opinion, reasons accounting for the social structure of human beings are of a deeper nature. They are based upon the fact that a belief 'is unlikely to occur as belief of individuals or particular groups'. Not being an idea or an opinion, a belief 'will normally be of a collective nature'[1]. Now, in spite of watering down this statement by means of the word 'normally', we cannot fail to be impressed by Ortega's insistence on the weight of social ties if we remember the deep significance of the word 'belief' in his vocabulary. Must we therefore conclude that the social element is the most powerful of all elements in the human being? We are prone to give an affirmative answer when we consider Ortega's treatment of the problem of social concord. In his opinion, society cannot subsist for long when dissent, instead of being an outcome of the strength and vitality of the body politic, affects the basic layers of common belief. When there is no consent in certain ultimate matters, and in particular when there is no agreement as to who shall rule, society dissolves and fundamental concord is replaced by fundamental dissent. It appears, in short, that Ortega ties up belief with social belief, leaving the destiny of the individual to the mercy of the destiny of society.

On the other hand, Ortega constantly points out that society is only the organization and collectivization of uses and opinions formerly held by individuals. He goes so far in this direction as to explain social activities as the inert result of spontaneous personal behaviour. Thus, for example, philosophy as a function in collective life, i.e., as a social fact backed by universities, pub-

[1] VI, 61 (1940) [*Concord*, p. 19].

lishers, etc., is the consequence of philosophy as a creative personal activity. Thus also the function of being a Caesar—at times an almost impersonal function—became possible because there was a man named 'Caesar' who possessed enough political genius to discover that a certain vacuum of power had to be filled by means of a new type of rule: so-called 'Caesarism'. Examples could easily be multiplied. All of them, however, would confirm the fact that society is never original and creative, that it limits itself to organizing and to administering previous original creations[1]. In other words, social usages are the *tardy* outcome of spontaneous forms of personal life. But this means that social forms bear the same relation to personal forms as the bark of the tree bears to its stem and even to its sap. Society is, as it were, the petrification of personality. No wonder Ortega has often spoken of the 'tyranny of society'[2]. No wonder too that he has even defined society as an 'irresponsible *ego*', as the omnipotence and omnipresence of the 'one'—the ever present '*one* says', '*one* hears', '*one* does'. The 'social mode' is defined accordingly as an inauthentic albeit an inevitable mode[3]. Therefore we must be careful not to confuse what automatically belongs to us and what merely belongs to the 'one' in us. We must, in short, be prepared to recognize that although estrangement is inevitable for the human being, he must always strive for withdrawal into himself[4].

It has been suggested that the above difficulties spring from Ortega's growing concern with spontaneity and authenticity. Filled with enthusiasm for the struggle against estrangement and falsification, the Spanish philosopher seems to have attached but little importance to what German thinkers have called 'the objective mind'. His remarks on how difficult or, in his vocabulary, how problematic and illusory it is to bear somebody else company provide a further confirmation of the above zeal for the authenticity of the self[5]. It is improbable, however, that Ortega himself has not been struck by these difficulties. Several attempts to clarify further his doctrine of society may be considered as a proof of his concern with such embarrassing questions.

[1] V, 174 (1934); V, 232 (1935); VI, 38 (1936) [*Toward*, p. 210]; VI, 395–9 (1940) [*Concord*, pp. 103–7].
[2] II, 745–48 (1930) [*Invertebrate Spain*, pp. 166–171]; V, 201–5 (1935).
[3] VI, 400 (1942) [*Concord*, p. 109].
[4] V, 60, 61, 74 (1933); V, 293–315 (1939).
[5] V, 61 (1933).

First, Ortega warns his readers that the expression 'man is a social being' is true only in a certain measure. As a matter of fact, man's social dispositions are constantly matched by his anti-social impulses[1]. Here lies, be it said in passing, the explanation of Ortega's paradoxical statement, 'Society is utopia'. For society does not work with the precision of a good watch; it usually works deplorably and lamentably. Second, collective life appears as a pure falsification only when we forget that every social fact is interlocked with other social facts and, therefore, when we omit to emphasize that a given society must be taken as a whole, each of its functions presupposing, and being presupposed by others. Third, and most important of all, society must not be confused with what Ortega calls 'the fact of living together', 'the fact of living with the rest', 'human coexistence'—*convivencia*. True, he did assert on one occasion that 'coexistence and society are equivalent terms'[2]. But he made it clear immediately afterwards that society must not be confused with association[3]. Thus human coexistence is not sufficient to make up a society[4]. Individuals may live together without necessarily bringing forth social rules and norms. This is the case with the most 'personal' of human relations: love, friendship, perhaps ties of kinship. In other words, a distinction must be introduced not only between collective or social life and personal life but also between social relationship and personal relationship. Social relations are based upon uses and rules. Personal relations are based upon spontaneity and authenticity. True, personal relationship may become social when it lasts a certain time or when certain conditions are given. But even then a difference persists. Will not this difference provide the missing link between pure authenticity and radical estrangement? We are not sure in the least whether Ortega would have accepted this as a solution to the above difficulties. At any rate, it is undeniable that without a close-knit analysis of what we may call inter-personal relationship Ortega's theory of society might run the risk of formalism—a risk that he has always consistently and painstakingly tried to avoid.

(d) The idea of philosophy

Philosophers have tackled many problems. But the most disturbing one has always been the problem of philosophy itself. What is philosophy? Is it a necessity? Is it a luxury? Is it a rigorous

[1] VI, 72–3 (1940) [*Concord*, pp. 24–5].
[2] IV, 117 (1930) [*Toward*, p. 49].
[3] *loc. cit.* [*Toward*, p. 50].
[4] VI, 38 (1936) [*Toward*, p. 211].

science? Is it an unwarranted set of assumptions? Implicitly or explicitly, many great philosophers have been bewildered by these questions. In the last decades, furthermore, even a new philosophical discipline has loomed up: the 'philosophy of philosophy', to which Nietzsche and Dilthey, among others, have contributed many keen insights. Ortega is no exception to this trend. He has been aware that philosophy is not something we must take for granted but something we must justify and account for unceasingly. Accordingly, we shall conclude this book with a few remarks on Ortega's idea of philosophy.

This idea is intimately related to what has been said about human life and in particular about the relationship between human life and knowledge. The reader will probably remember that in Ortega's opinion knowledge is not the automatic release of psychological mechanisms but rather a human acquisition. Running counter to Aristotle's celebrated principle, 'All men by nature desire to know', he says, or rather implies, that if 'Man has a nature' is a preposterous saying, then 'Man has a knowing nature' is a senseless one. All things considered, however, it is easy to see that the word 'knowledge' in the above sense is irreparably ambiguous. On the one hand, knowledge is defined as a vital function. On the other hand, knowledge is considered *also* as a conventional cognitive process. How is one to account for the undeniable difference between the former and the latter? Ortega has come to think that a terminological device may cast some light on this tangled question. Let us introduce it here, for it will prove useful for an understanding of the meaning of philosophy, that is, of the rôle that philosophy plays or can play in human existence.

The device in question roughly consists in introducing a distinction between knowledge—or cognition—and thinking[1].

What is thinking? Like everything which has some bearing on human life, thinking does not appear to us in its 'naked truth'. It appears to us masked by all kinds of deceiving realities. The expression 'deceiving realities' must be understood in its full and literal sense: the realities masking the genuine phenomenon of 'thinking' are deceiving and confusing precisely because they are very similar to what they *pretend* to be without being it in the least. Among these concealing realities two deserve special mention. One is thinking as a psychological process; the other, thinking as a set of logical rules.

Thinking as a psychological process is open to the same objections already singled out when, after examining the meaning

[1] V, 517–47 (1941) [*Concord*, pp. 49–82].

61

of knowledge for human life, we concluded, following Ortega, that the question 'What is knowledge?'—now reformulated in the question 'What is thinking?'—cannot be answered by means of a description of the psychological mechanisms which make it possible for us to think. Psychological mechanisms are merely instrumental in the production of thinking, because in its primary sense thinking is the fact that we put those mechanisms *in use for* some purpose. Man must dedicate himself to thinking, *because* he has to free himself of doubts. Thinking takes on different forms, and what we call 'knowledge' or 'cognition' is only one among them. The fact that it is *for us* the outstanding form does not mean that it is the only possible one.

Another reality masking the genuine phenomenon of thinking is, according to Ortega, logic. It has been held that thinking is primarily logical thinking, namely, thinking according to certain rules—the very rules to which classical logicians have given the name of 'principles'. But logical thinking is, again, one among the many possible forms of thinking. In fact, it is a very restricted one. If the limitations of logical thinking had not been discovered earlier, it was because philosophers had shown an unbounded confidence in a certain type of logic. Implicitly or explicitly the assumption had been made that the principles of classical logic were the only trustworthy guiding norms of human thought. This confidence was shaken as soon as it was discovered that the foundations of traditional logic can no longer rely upon the ontological assumptions predominant for more than two thousand years in the history of Western philosophy. Like the foundations of all sciences, the foundations of logic—and of mathematics—have undergone a momentous, and healthy, crisis. Mathematical logic in particular has shown that old concepts such as 'principle', 'truth' and so on must be drastically revised. Indeed alternative logics are nowadays held possible. Thinking must not, therefore, be confused with logical thinking, inasmuch as the expression 'logical thinking' has lost most, if not all, of its traditional connotations.

If thinking is neither a psychological process nor a set of logical rules, it will no longer be plausible to say that it is always a cognitive act. Thinking has thus a broader meaning than knowledge. In fact, knowledge is only *one* form in the rich morphology of thinking. And as neither psychology nor logic nor, for that matter, philosophy or science, can tell us what knowledge is, we are compelled to look elsewhere for an answer to our question. This answer we find, according to Ortega, in that element permeating all human reality: history.

The phenomenon we call 'knowledge' or 'cognition', namely, the particular way of thinking that makes use of concepts and of reasoned analyses and arguments, has come out at a certain stage of man's historical development. When? Only when certain presuppositions had been fulfilled. Ortega mentions two of them: (1) the belief that behind the chaos of impressions there is a stable reality called the 'being' of things, and (2) the belief that human intellect is the sole possibility of grasping the nature of such a stable reality. Now, it is commonly agreed that only the Greek philosophers held these beliefs in a sufficiently radical manner. The circumstances that prompted Greek philosophers to reach them would require considerably more space than is available here. Let it suffice to point out that, as is always the case with human life, the Greeks arrived at those beliefs because some other previous beliefs had been shaken to their foundations. Thus the Greek philosophers became, as Ortega puts it, 'cognizers' *par excellence*. They transmitted to us a splendid heritage which we have since spent lavishly. As a consequence, the idea has been held for more than two thousand years that cognition and, therefore, philosophy as a purely cognitive activity, are something man can always lay hands on, and accordingly scarcely in need of special justification. The use of concepts and of reasoned arguments has become so 'natural' in our Western culture, and in the areas influenced by it, that we have come to the conclusion that philosophical activity is, so to speak, inborn and can be easily cultivated by means of proper education. The philosophers in particular have often wondered how it is possible for some people to dispense altogether with philosophy, the 'non-philosophical existence' being, in their opinion, far less complete and endurable than the philosophical one. These thinkers have, in short, taken philosophy for granted and have paid little or no attention to the very motives from which philosophy itself springs.

Now to be a 'cognizer' is by no means something connatural with human existence. There have been, and there still exist, many types of men who, for better or for worse, do not place on cognition the emphasis which has been matter of course in Western culture. A case in point is the Hebrew way of life before any contact with cognitive cultures had been established. The Hebrews believed, for instance, that reality was identical with God—with a God who was pure will, arbitrary power, having in principle no relation whatsoever with what we call the rules of morality or the laws of nature. Such rules and laws, if they existed at all, were a pure mercy of God that God could withdraw with the same facility—and incomprehensibility—as He bestowed them. Everything that happened to the human creature depended, therefore, upon the inscrutable decrees of God. How in this case was one to adopt a cognitive attitude? It would be entirely useless. In the face of that overwhelming God prayer is far more rewarding and even far more enlightening than reason. No wonder prayer becomes in that case a form of thinking, having its own technique and its own rules. But this changes not only the fundamental ways of life but also the meaning of certain terms. It changes, for instance, the meaning of the word 'truth'. What we call 'truth' is then no longer the discovery of the stable being hidden behind the unstable appearances of reality; it is the 'discovery' of what God might have decided or the understanding of what God might have revealed. Let us call this discovery by its proper name: prophecy. In other words, what we call a 'true statement' will not be, as it was among the Greek philosophers, a 'description' of 'what really is' but an announcement of 'what it will really be'.

Some other examples might, of course, be quoted. As a matter of fact, a careful description of the main features of Western culture would show that even this culture has not always given cognition a free hand. But the above example, being considerably more extreme than many others, will help the reader to understand that while man cannot escape thinking as a way of getting along with the difficulties of his life, he is able, and above all he *has been* able, to solve the riddles of his life by means other than knowledge. Whether this is desirable or even possible in the present stage of history is, of course, another question—and a very difficult one, indeed. We cannot here dwell on this problem, nor can we raise and still less debate the question of whether the meaning of the propositions upheld by science or philosophy can be reduced to the rôle that science or philosophy as such play in human existence. Even if this reduction proves impossible, it remains undeniable that Ortega's historical idea of knowledge and his subsequent historical account of philosophy may cast a vivid light on certain aspects of both that have been deplorably neglected. At any event, what philosophers can learn from Ortega is that 'the first principle of a philosophy is the justification of itself'. Ortega himself never lost sight of this necessity.

ORTEGA Y GASSET'S WORKS

(Only books are listed. Dates refer to the first printing.)

Meditaciones del Quijote, 1914.
Vieja y nueva política, 1914.
Personas, obras, cosas, 1916.
El Espectador, I, 1916.
El Espectador, II, 1917.
El Espectador, III, 1921.
España invertebrada. Bosquejo de algunos pensamientos históricos, 1921.
El tema de nuestro tiempo. El ocaso de las revoluciones. El sentido histórico de la teoría de Einstein, 1923.
Las Atlántidas, 1924.
La deshumanización del arte e ideas sobre la novela, 1925.
El Espectador, IV, 1925.
El Espectador, V, 1927.
El Espectador, VI, 1927.
Espíritu de la letra, 1927.
Tríptico. I. Mirabeau o el político, 1927.
Notas, 1928.
El Espectador, VII, 1929.
Kant (17241924).i Reflexiones de centenario, 1929.
Misión de la Unversidad, 1930.
La rebelión de las masas, 1930.
Rectificación de la República, 1931.
La redención de las provincias y la decencia nacional, 1931.
Goethe desde dentro, 1933.
El Espectador, VIII, 1934.
Ensimismamiento y alteración. Meditación de la técnica, 1939.
El libro de las misiones, 1940 (includes Misión de la Universidad).
Ideas y creencias, 1940.
Estudios sobre el amor, 1940 (includes some essays published in earlier books).
Mocedades, 1941 (includes some essays published in Personas, obras, cosas).
Historia como sistema y Del Imperio Romano, 1941.
Teoría de Andalucía y otros ensayos, 1942.
Esquema de las crisis, 1942.
Dos prólogos. A un tratado de montería. A una historia de la filosofía, 1945.
Papeles sobre Velázquez y Goya, 1950.

Forthcoming posthumous works:
El hombre y la gente.
La idea de principio y Leibniz.
¿ Qué es filosofía ?.

CONTENTS OF 'OBRAS COMPLETAS'

Vol. I

Pp. 11–264 *Artículos (1902–1913).*
265–308 *Vieja y nueva política (1914).*
309–400 *Meditaciones del Quijote (1914).*
401–416 *Artículos (1915).*
417–574 *Personas, obras, cosas (1916).*

Vol. II

Pp. 13–748 *El Espectador,* Vols. I-VIII *(1916–1934).*

Vol. III

Pp. 9–34 *Artículos (1917–1920).*
35–128 *España invertebrada (1921).*
129–140 *Artículos (1923).*
141–242 *El tema de nuestro tiempo (1923).*
243–280 *Artículos (1924).*
281–316 *Las Atlántidas (1924).*
317–336 *Epílogo al libro 'De Francesca a Beatrice' (1924).*
337–349 *Artículos (1925).*
351–428 *La deshumanización del arte (1925).*
429–510 *Artículos (1926–1927).*
511–599 *Espíritu de la letra (1927).*
601–637 *Mirabeau o el político (1927).*

Vol. IV

Pp. 9–21 *Artículos (1929).*
23–59 *Kant (1929).*
61–109 *Artículos (1930).*
111–310 *La rebelión de las masas (1930).*
311–353 *Misión de la Universidad (1930).*
355–379 *Artículos (1931–1932).*
381–541 *Goethe desde dentro (1932).*
543–554 *Artículos (1933).*

Vol. V

Pp. 9–164 *En torno a Galileo (1933).*
165–206 *Artículos (1934–1935).*
207–234 *Misión del bibliotecario (1935).*
235–287 *Artículos (1935–1937).*
289–375 *Ensimismamiento y alteración (1939).*
377–489 *Ideas y creencias (1940).*
491–626 *Artículos (1940–1941).*

Vol. VI

Pp. 9–107 *Historia como sistema y Del Imperio Romano (1941).*
109–214 *Teoría de Andalucía y otros ensayos (1942).*
215–244 *Brindis (1917–1939).*
245–512 *Prólogos (1914–1943).*

ENGLISH TRANSLATIONS

The Modern Theme. Translated by James Cleugh. London: C. W. Daniel, 1941. New York: W. W. Norton, 1933.

The Revolt of the Masses. Authorized translation. London: Allen & Unwin, 1923. New York: W. W. Norton, 1932. Often reprinted.

Invertebrate Spain. Translated by Mildred Adams. New York: W. W. Norton, 1937.

Contents:

Pp. 19–87: 'Invertebrate Spain' (some passages of the original Spanish edition have been deleted).

Pp. 88–102: 'A theory about Andalusia'. A translation of an article originally published in 1927 and reprinted in *Teoría de Andalucía y otros ensayos* and in *O.C.*, VI, 111–120.

Pp. 103–115: 'Castile and the Asturias'. A translation of parts of 'De Madrid a Asturias o los dos paisajes', originally published in 1915 and reprinted in *El Espectador*, III and in *O.C.*, II, 249–265.

Pp. 116–142: 'The Meaning of Castles in Spain'. A translation of parts of 'Notas del vago estío', originally published in 1925 and reprinted in *El Espectador*, V and in *O.C.*, II, 413–450.

Pp. 143–157: 'A Topography of Spanish Pride'. A translation of parts of 'Para una topografía de la soberbia española (Breve análisis de una pasión)', originally published in 1923 and reprinted in *Goethe desde dentro* and in *O.C.*, IV, 459–466.

Pp. 158–165: 'Arid Plains, and Arid Men'. A translation of parts of 'Temas de viaje (Julio de 1922)', reprinted in *El Espectador*, IV and in *O.C.*, II, 367–383.

Pp. 166–171: 'The Increasing Menace of Society'. A translation of the article 'Socialización del hombre', originally published in 1930 and reprinted in *El Espectador*, VIII and in *O.C.*, II, 745–748.

Pp. 172–189: 'Against the Economic Interpretation of History'. A translation of 'La interpretación bélica de la historia', originally published in 1925 and reprinted in *El Espectador*, VI and in *O.C.*, II, 525–536.

Pp. 190–201: 'On Fascism'. A translation of 'Sobre el fascismo', originally published in 1925 and reprinted in *El Espectador*, VI and in *O.C.*, II, 497–505.

Pp. 202–212: 'Meditation in the Escorial'. A translation of parts of 'Meditación del Escorial', originally published in 1915 and reprinted in *El Espectador*, VI and in *O.C.*, II, 553–560.

Toward a Philosophy of History. New York: W. W. Norton, 1941.

Contents:

Pp. 11–40: 'The Sportive Origin of the State', translated by Helene Weyl from 'El origen deportivo del Estado', originally published in 1924 and reprinted in *El Espectador*, VII and in *O.C.*, 607–623.

Pp. 41-83: 'Unity and Diversity of Europe', reprinted from Eleanor Clark's translation of 'Prólogo para franceses' (1937), included in a

new edition of *La rebelión de las masas* and in *O.C.*, IV, 113–139.
Pp. 85–161: 'Man the Technician', translated by Helene Weyl from *Meditación de la técnica*, a series of lectures given in 1933, published in *Ensimismamiento y alteración* and in *O.C.*, V, 317–375.
Pp. 163–233: 'History as a System', reprinted from William C. Atkinson's translation of 'Historia como sistema', originally published (in English translation) in *Philosophy and History. Essays presented to Ernst Cassirer*, edited by Raymond Klibansky and H. J. Paton. Oxford: Clarendon Press, 1936, pp. 283–322. The Spanish text was published later in *Historia como sistema y Del Imperio Romano*, and has been reprinted in *O.C.*, VI, 11–50.
Pp. 235–273: 'The Argentine State and the Argentinean', translated by Helene Weyl from 'El hombre a la defensiva', originally published in 1929 and reprinted in *El Espectador*, VII and in *O.C.*, II, 643–666.

Mission of the University. Translated by Howard Lee Nostrand. Princeton: Princeton University Press, 1944. London: K. Paul Trench, Trubner 1946.

Concord and Liberty. Translated by Helene Weyl. New York: W. W. Norton, 1946.

Contents:

Pp. 9–47: 'Concord and Liberty'. A translation of 'Del Imperio Romano', a series of articles originally published in 1940 and reprinted in *Historia como sistema y Del Imperio Romano* and in *O.C.*, VI, 51–107.
Pp. 49–82: 'Notes on Thinking—Its Creation of the World and Its Creation of God'. A translation of 'Apuntes sobre el pensamiento: su teurgia y su demiurgia', originally published in 1941 and reprinted in *O.C.*, V, 517–546.
Pp. 83–128: 'Prologue to a History of Philosophy'. A translation of a long preface to the Spanish translation of E. Bréhier's *Histoire de la philosophie*. Ortega's 'Prólogo' was originally published in 1942 and has been reprinted in *Dos Prólogos* and in *O.C.*, VI, 377–418.
Pp. 129–182: 'A Chapter from the History of Ideas. Wilhelm Dilthey and the Idea of Life'. A translation of 'Guillermo Dilthey y la idea de la vida', originally published in 1933–1934, reprinted in *Teoría de Andalucía y otros ensayos* and in *O.C.*, VI, 165–214.

The Dehumanization of Art and Notes on the Novel. Translated by Helene Weyl. Princeton: Princeton University Press, 1948. Reprinted New York: P. Smith, 1948.

Among English translations of articles not published in book form, we mention as philosophically relevant:
'In Search of a Goethe from within', *The Partisan Review*, Vol. XVI, No. 12, December, 1949, pp. 116–188. Translated by Willard R. Trask. 'Believing and Thinking', *Essays and Studies by Students of Simmons College*, Vol. XI, No. 1, November, 1952, pp. 1–6. Translation completed under the direction of Professor Edith F. Helman.

BIOGRAPHICAL NOTE

1883   Born Madrid, May 9th.

1898–1902 Student at the Universidad Central (University of Madrid). Took degree of Licenciado en Filosofía y Letras. Previous studies of Bachillerato in Colegio de Jesuítas de Miraflores del Palo (Málaga) and one year in Deusto.

1904   Took doctor's degree in the University of Madrid with a dissertation entitled *Los terrores del año mil (Crítica de una leyenda).*

1905–1907 Post-graduate studies in Germany: Leipzig, Berlin and Marburg.

1910   Professor of Metaphysics in the University of Madrid (until 1936).

1915   Founded *España*, in cooperation with some other writers.

1916   Lectures in Argentina.

1917   Gave up writing articles for *El Imparcial*. Associated with the new periodical *El Sol*.

1923   Founded *Revista de Occidente*. Publication suspended in 1936, but books by Ediciones de la Revista de Occidente are still being published.

1931   Founded Agrupación al Servicio de la República (with R. Pérez de Ayala and G. Marañón). Delegate at the Chamber of Deputies (Cortes Constituyentes). Ceased to contribute to *El Sol* and began writing articles for *Crisol* and *Luz*.

1936–1945 Residence in France, Holland, Argentina, Portugal.

1945–1954 Residence in Spain and Portugal, with frequent trips and residence abroad.

1948   Founded in Madrid, with Julián Marías, the *Instituto de Humanidades*, a private institution.

1949   Lectures in the U.S.

1949–1951 Lectures in Germany and Switzerland.

1951   Doctor *honoris causa*, University of Glasgow.

1955   Died Madrid, October 18th.

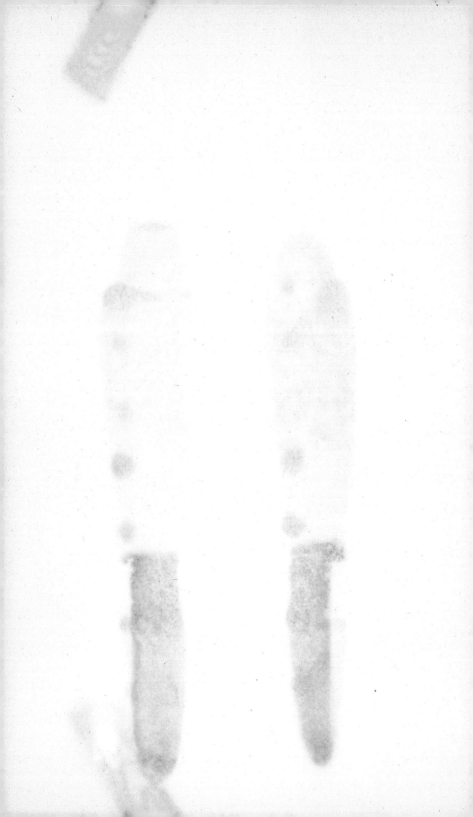